Diving Deep
to Climb High

You are so much more extra ordinary than you were meant to believe.

Frances
xx

Diving Deep *to* Climb High

Helping women in business to see,
that what lies beneath, is a direct
reflection of their own self-worth

Frances Day

Copyright Year: 2023

Copyright Notice: by Frances Day of Wise Women Publishing.

All rights reserved.

The above information forms this copyright notice: © 2023 by Frances Day of Wise Women Publishing. All rights reserved.

ISBN 978-1-7394551-0-1 – Paperback
ISBN 978-1-7394551-1-8 – Ebook

This book goes out to every woman in business who is creative, sells her services, and helps other women to be the best version of themselves. Those who sometimes wonder if running their own business is the best way to live their lives.

To all women that have gone before me, helping me to get to this place of freedom and self-realisation.

Big thanks to Beverly Hopper for her undiluted gift of giving and for her hours of support in helping me give birth to this book.

Also, a great big hug of gratitude to Lynn Robinson for sharing her spiritual gifts with me and supporting me on my journey.

And finally to Sheridan Leigh my Soul Sister, for her love and support.

I love you all.

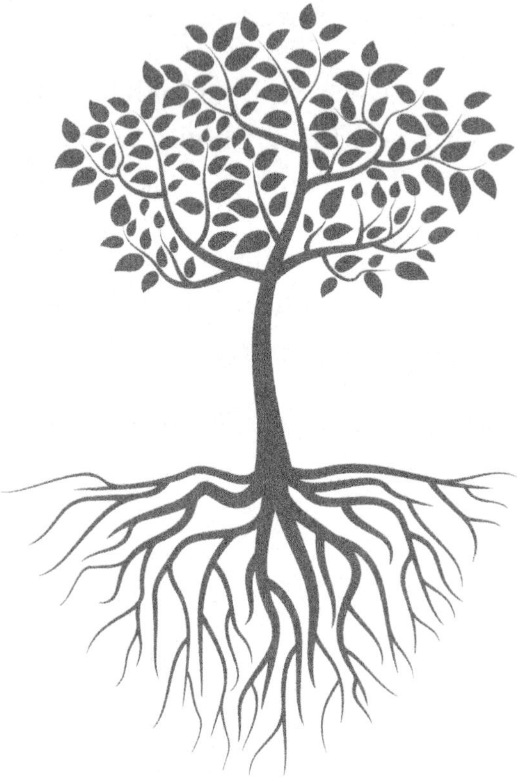

CONTENTS

Introduction   1

1. The kindness of strangers   15
2. Everything happens for a reason   39
3. Learning to listen to your inner voice and not someone else's
   opinions   47
4. See how The Universe reflects at you what you're thinking   51
5. Masculine and Feminine Energy   65
6. Money is masculine energy   71
7. Self worth and my dating experiences   81
8. Let the healing begin   139
9. Victim, or priestess - you choose   149
10. Searching for more Joy in my life   157
11. Setting up a smart business   161
12. Finding your GIFT - everyone has a gift and a medicine   169
13. Client Stories   173

Epilogue   187
Acknowledgments   191
Additional Resources   193
Bibliography   195
About the Author   197

Introduction

Are you attracting negative experiences into your life?

Do you feel like you're going round and round in circles whilst you're watching other women, who seem to have it all? From the outside, they've got the nice guy, and a successful business, and everything seems to be going from strength to strength for them, in every area of their lives.

And do you catch yourself thinking, 'Why do I never seem to be able to get a break?'

Perhaps you've already run a business, and for some reason, it just didn't take off.

The reason is not because of anything you've done wrong, it's because of your self-worth.

Self-worth is something that is a learned behaviour. Perhaps because of a challenging childhood, or something that's been passed down through your DNA lineage.

The only way that you're going to stop these negative life experiences, is by doing the internal work.

You owe this to your family and mostly yourself, to create a life that you truly deserve.

Imagine if by doing the internal work you come out of the other side, improved, and more successful than you've ever been in life and business.

Imagine if by doing the work, and diving deep, you discover that you have limiting beliefs that sit beneath the surface that you didn't even know existed.

Hundreds of years ago, women were the most powerful force. Men sought us out for our wisdom and healing powers, but then the tables turned and around the 1600s, witch hunting was at its peak. Men felt threatened by our power and decided that they wanted to rule. A little like all the wars that still happen today. Man claiming territory and fighting for supremacy and power.

These women, one by one, were persecuted, hung, and drowned because they threatened masculine supremacy.

These wounds, limiting beliefs, wounded child stories, and energetic blocks sit in our DNA and past lifetimes, and still, today, they keep us playing small.

Limiting beliefs show up when we don't believe that we can do something, but the mind is very powerful. It limits us, from stepping into the woman that we are meant to be. Wounded child stories stem from our childhood, as the name suggests. From the age of zero to two, we are sponges, soaking up lots of information in our brand-new world. We learn more in those first two years than at any other time in our lives, and not just logical brain things. We learn what it is to be human with the subtle, emotional context of interactions with our family unit. The problem comes when we lack positive role models.

Energetic blocks are a little more subtle than the previous two. Emotions are energy in motion. When we experience a negative event in life, large or small, if we don't release it within 3 – 6 months, it becomes stuck in our body. This can then cause dis-ease. If we don't deal with the negative emotion, they may manifest themselves in the short term, or as the years progress become more intense.

When we release this energy, we step into our true calling with ease and grace and an inner knowing that we are on the right path.

For example, imagine that you're online dating. And every guy you ever meet is just not the right type for you. This was what happened to me. You're energetically attracting a similar type because of your energetic vibration. I talk about this further on in the book, and as lots of coaches say, 'You just don't know what you don't know.'

When we have spent all our lives, mostly on autopilot, we don't know that there is a better way to live our lives. It's not until you shift the energy and see it from a new perspective that you see how your patterns were playing out.

Language has energy, and as that potential suitor reads your online profile, he'll make an informed decision about whether you're a match for him. We make decisions on so many levels, not just visually, but energetically too.

And if he had a traumatic past, then you will subliminally attract that to yourself too. It's not until you do the deep transformative work that you truly see what you were doing.

In this book, I share my story, not to throw a pity party, but so that you get a better understanding of how you, as a woman, are conditioned, year after year. Generation after generation, to be kind, to give, to support, and nurture.

Sharing my personal story has helped me heal. When I was in the thick of it, living that life, I had no idea that I was the one that was attracting these situations into my life. I was playing the victim. (I talk in more detail about victim level further into the book.) I now know that I had to go through these experiences so that I could help other women to heal their wounds. We naturally want to nurture, be giving, and be supportive, but so often there is a conditioning placed upon us which goes beyond that which nature intended. Too often we women have an expectation placed upon us which results in us being the rock on which others rely to become successful. This often leaves us questioning our self-worth and resulting in feelings of unfulfillment and anxiety.

You've heard the sayings…

Don't be so bossy.

Who do you think you are?

Be a good girl.

I don't think you deserve that.

Know your place.

Don't be selfish.

You heard all these statements from your parents or primary caregivers, and let's be honest, they were only doing the best they could with what they had. There's no blame or accusation here.

Our female ancestors fought for our equal rights so that we and our daughters could have all that we deserve, the same as men have come to accept it as a God-given right. And even though, on the surface, we appear to have it all, we're still, at a deep level, playing small, because of the conditioning that sits in our DNA. These beliefs have been passed from one generation to another.

By sharing my story, I hope that it will help you to see that it's always an inside job. That what lies beneath the surface is our true self. You may show up on the surface as a confident woman in business, but the real woman is a representation of that little girl that sits beneath the surface and just wants approval and to be loved.

We may show up with a big smile, looking confident for all the world to see, but if what lies beneath the surface is a broken little girl, that little girl will always be in the driving seat.

Who is this book for?

It's for you if you run your own business. Because your business has a clever way of being able to reflect, what's going on beneath the surface for you. It's for you if you know that you have a purpose in life and want to know how to use those experiences to create a positive impact. It's for you if you have had a challenging life and need tools to help you work through these challenges in the privacy of your own space. It's for you if you want to change family patterns. If you want to know that you're not on your own. That you do have a voice. That you can make a difference.

Everything is energy, so what you believe on the inside, reflects on the outside. Your conscious mind knows that you need to charge higher prices. That you should show up confidently, with a product or service that's different from everyone else. You may know your industry like the back of your hand, but if your self-worth isn't aligned, then your self-worth equates to your self-worth. This means that you'll only ever earn what you feel you deserve.

There's no point masking it, and carrying on regardless, because sooner or later, it will catch up with you, and I share this in my story. Only by diving deep will you be able to climb high.

You may find that it brings up things that you'd rather forget. You may find that it makes you feel uncomfortable. I promise, that by bringing them to the surface energetically, and letting them go, you'll feel a whole lot better.

You are human, and the thing that makes you, your beautiful self, is your emotions. When those emotions get trapped in your energy system, they can cause dis-ease. The work that you do now, will help you with your four energy systems. Mental, physical, emotional, and spiritual. To give you a fully rounded, optimal you.

No matter why you choose to read this book, I hope you approach it with playful curiosity. Please read it that way. Ask yourself, 'How can this woman's story help me to see the patterns in my life? What experiences am I attracting? How can I break the ties from my past and use them to create a life that I deserve?'

We will go deeper, to help you see with absolute clarity, what your subconscious is reflecting at you.

So how does it work?

To help you understand in more detail, I've structured the book into three categories.

Firstly, I'm going to share the theory of why it works this way.

Second, I'll share my story with you, to show you the patterns, that I couldn't see whilst I was in the thick of it.

Thirdly, I'll give you some tools to help you to see.

    a. What the patterns are.

    b. How you're attracting these experiences.

    c. Help you to break the cycles. For good!

Why me?

I write this book in my 60th year. And all my life, I attracted the wrong men. They all looked very different. Some were rich, some poor as church mice, but all had similar issues.

I married twice and had one real love of my life.

I've been well off. Had successful businesses. I've lost it all, and I wish I'd known then what I know now, I would have lived my life very differently.

I needed someone to confide in, who could give me wise advice about my businesses and my relationships. You think that they're separate entities, but they're not, because everything is connected.

I've run a few different businesses. A tiny sandwich round, a marketing agency, and a successful woman coaching business. But the bigger I got, the harder I fell, and I lost it all. I wasn't dealing with what was going on beneath the surface.

What was the common theme? Me. My self-worth. And it wasn't until 2018, when I discovered energy healing, that I learned how to heal myself. It's probably the gentlest, and yet most effective way of healing that I have ever come across. I didn't need to talk to anyone about it. To be a good healer, you need to have healed yourself. And by doing this I've realised how powerful we are.

Writing this book has helped me heal. It's also reinforced that helping women heal is my purpose in life. I felt that I had to share my story, so that women like you, would benefit from my experiences.

What are you going to learn?

You'll learn more about yourself than you've ever learned before. You'll see that it's always an inside job. You'll learn that you're the creator of your life.

Whatever has happened in the past, is there, in the past. You have the power to change everything. You get to call the shots because what lies beneath the surface, is not who you're meant to be.

You've picked up this book because you know at some level something is not working for you.

This book will take you deep. At the end of most chapters, there are exercises to help you discover what lies beneath the surface.

And once your conscious mind sees this, you'll understand why you repeat the same actions.

Your subconscious mind drives 80% of your decision-making process. It makes sense to see what lies beneath.

Chapter One - The Kindness of Strangers.

I share some of my story, where on one fateful night, my life became so intolerable, that I had to finally do something about it.

Chapter Two - Everything Happens for a Reason.

I go right back to the beginning so that you can see where it all began. Plus, I'll share the theory behind secondary gain stories. We all have them, but the more intelligent we are, the trickier they are to find.

Chapter Three - Learning to Listen to Your Inner Voice.

I share the final part of the fallout of my business and how I had to listen to what I was being told. I had no option.

Chapter Four – The Universe Reflects What You're Thinking.

I give you a task, to look at what's going on for you. Read the previous chapters first so that you get an understanding of what may be the underlying factors. Plus, where it all began. I share the story of my childhood.

Chapter Five - Masculine and Feminine Energy.

With examples of how it can be optimal or distorted, to give you an extra layer of recognition about what may be going on for you.

Chapter Six - Money is Masculine Energy

My favourite subject. Money. How money is masculine energy and I give you tools to help you see where you may be playing small.

Chapter Seven – Self worth and my dating experiences.

If your experiences are less than optimal in the dating game, then this chapter is for you. It's an absolute revelation.

Chapter Eight – Let the Healing Begin.

I find a way out of the deep routed trauma that's been running around in my energy system.

Chapter Nine - Victim, or Priestess.

You choose.

I share some more tools to help you to see what lies beneath the surface so you can start your healing journey.

Chapter Ten - Searching for more Joy in my life.

I share with you a life-changing event that connected me at all four levels. Mental, physical, emotional, and spiritual.

Chapter Eleven – Setting up a Smart Business

This starts with my first job and how that influenced my opinion of working for men. I'll help you see that the way you set up your business, will give it longevity. Plus, you'll gain the freedom that you deserve. And finally, a great process for having tough conversations. I call it the three 'F' formula.

Chapter Twelve – Finding Your Gift

With every experience, there is a lesson.

Chapter Thirteen – Client Stories

To show you how a shift in energy can change the way that you show up in the world.

The writing of my book has been one of the processes that has helped me heal. Once I realised that I could use my experiences to help other women, it changed my momentum completely. I had a bigger reason than just me, to get it out into the world. Once this realisation hit me, I completed the book in a much shorter time. One of the reasons for writing this book is to let you know that you're not alone. That you have a great big band of sisters, who are there for you. Encouraging you, every step of the way.

As low self-worth sits in your energy system, it cascades through every part of your life.

Even if you think that you're ok on a conscious level, this distorted energy may be so deeply buried that you don't even know it is there.

I've created a download for you. My gift to you.

If you'd like to explore what lies beneath the surface for you.

Simply copy the link below to take you to
subscribepage.io/selfworthexercise

Buy yourself a beautiful journal and use it to explore what lies beneath the surface. Because by diving deep, you'll climb high beautiful girl.

Take your time. Read the stories. Do the tasks. I'd love to know if they've helped you in any way.

If you'd like to connect, you can find me below.
Facebook https://www.facebook.com/FrancesDayCoach
Instagram https://www.instagram.com/francesdaycoach/
LinkedIn https://www.linkedin.com/in/francesdayceo/

Finally, be hopeful.

The only way to change the way that you show up in the world is to do the internal work.

As Einstein said, 'Insanity is doing the same thing over and over again and expecting different results.'

Let the healing begin.

CHAPTER ONE

The kindness of strangers

On the night that Princess Diana died I was being held from a 9th Floor flat window by a man I thought loved me.

The morning after, I was laying on my mum's couch, having gone through the most horrendous experience of my life.

That was 31st August 1997. It was Bank Holiday weekend, and my mum and stepdad were away for the weekend.

I recognised I was at a point in my life where I thought, "This has got to stop!" Although it's 25 years since it happened, at the time of writing this story, it feels like yesterday.

When you have no control over whether you live or die, and you find yourself laughing hysterically, as you are hanging out of the window, and your life is hanging by a thread, it gives you the great big wake-up call that you need.

I'd met this man whilst I was working locally in a pub. He was a tree surgeon, and very handsome. The kind of man who could take your breath away as he walked through the door with his immaculate physique and dashing good looks. Carrying strong upper body strength that he needed to climb trees; he had muscles underneath his arms that I didn't even know existed.

He used to call into the pub where I was working. In the beginning, he was quite shy, but, over the weeks we got to know one another. I noticed once he'd had a couple of drinks his confidence grew. He worked for the council and had recently split up from his wife. I could see that he was going through a bit of a tough time. Under the surface there was a vulnerability about him, that I found endearing like a little boy lost.

He introduced me to a friend of his, who had recently split up from his wife, and he had a free holiday to Tenerife up for grabs. All I had to do was pay the £20 transfer fee for the ticket. I grabbed it with both hands. At that time, I'd managed to secure a full-time job at a design agency and had to beg the boss to take two weeks off. As you can imagine, it was a very boozy holiday. His friend was getting over the breakup with his previous partner, and we were in a new relationship, and just getting to know one another.

One of the strongest memories that I have of that holiday is sitting on the balcony of the apartment in the early hours of the morning singing songs from the shows with his friend.

The tree surgeon had of course already gone to bed because he'd started drinking way too early. I got on better with his friend than I did with my new boyfriend, but then of course my self-esteem was so low that I couldn't see that at the time. I'd just managed to get a cheap council flat in town. The rent was low, and just starting out, I needed something to get me started. He was sleeping on his mum's couch, so it was inevitable that we moved in together quite quickly after the holiday.

It was too soon, as I did not know him well enough. I knew he liked drinking. He used to drink Stella, but what I hadn't seen before we started living together was how it affected him. He would drink every day. And if he wasn't going to the pub, he'd call off at the corner shop for a four-pack of Stella to drink at home. Stella is known as 'The Wife Beater' because there must be something in its chemical makeup that can send people into rage and anger. I guess a little like gin is reputed to make you feel sad.

I was happy. I'd found a man whom I was proud to call my partner. We were both working full-time and just getting on with life. One night we had arranged to go out with some friends to Halifax town center. I smoked cigarettes at the time and had bought a new packet. We finished our drinks in one pub and walked to another when I realised that I'd left my cigarettes on the table in the last pub.

At that time, they were about £5 per packet, which was a lot of money for me then, so I was fed up. My heart sank as I knew they wouldn't be there if we went back for them. Someone would have picked them up. But he had noticed when I'd left them behind and had picked them up. He pulled them out of his pocket, with a sneer on his face, and said, 'Got money to burn, have you?' He hated me smoking, and I witnessed this menacing dark mist descend on his face, which I'd seen once before.

During our holiday in Tenerife, I think he sensed that I got on better with his friend than him, and he'd got into a rage about me spending more time with his friend. He couldn't see that it was because he'd become so drunk that I preferred to spend time with his friend than him.

I was filled with dread. My mind started racing. I felt sick to my stomach. I knew that we were in for a night of arguing and falling out. The Wife Beater had kicked in. I thought, 'I'm not doing this again, he scares me when he's like this.' I gave my apologies to the couple and said, 'I'm going home. I don't feel well.'

It was about 9.30 pm. and I picked up my coat and started walking out of the door. The flats where we lived were about a mile away, so I wrapped up warm and started walking. I knew that he would follow me, but I had nowhere else to go. The flat was in my name, and I was going back to my home.

I heard his footsteps behind me, they were pounding on the street in unison with my heartbeat. Shortly after I walked through the door, I heard his key turn in the lock, and he walked into the living room. My heart was pounding, as I knew what was about to follow. We had an awful argument, about money, and for the life in me, I cannot remember the tiny detail. The rage in this man was off the scale. Then, out of nowhere, he started walking toward me. He picked me up, his eyes did not look like they truly saw me. Almost robotically, his face changed from the man that I thought I knew. I am 5 feet seven and not tiny at all, but the strength of this man was like the strength of ten men. I found myself hanging out of the window, hanging onto the window frame with all my might. I was hanging there thinking, I'm going to die. This man was so strong. Just one slip of his hand, and I'll drop from these nine floors up, onto the hard concrete below. I started laughing hysterically as tears streamed down my face. Surely this was not how my life would end?

Then just as quickly as it began, reality kicked in. He pulled me up, and the angry mist on his face lifted. It was as though he'd realised what he was about to do. I ran as fast as I could towards the door of the flat, but he dragged me back. He knocked me to the floor and held me by my arms on the floor, pinning me down. He had one of his steel-toe cap boots that he wore for work and banged it, with all his might right next to my face. He terrified me. I think that was the point. He wanted to make me so scared of him, that I would not fight back. But I don't think he knew who he was dealing with. He didn't know that I'd been through the terror of being beaten before and I vowed to myself it would never happen again. I was quite literally fighting for my life. I got away again and somehow, and I don't know how I managed to get out of the flat. Opposite my flat, lived an elderly couple. I banged on the door with all my might, and they let me in.

The poor old lady was scared because she told me that her husband had a weak heart, and she didn't want anything to upset him. I said that I needed to use her phone to call the police and I'd be on my way.

When the two police officers arrived, they asked me to explain what had happened and then asked if they could access the flat to talk to him. Now here's the interesting part. Because the flat was in my name, he showed me how to open the door from the outside, even though it was locked. They told me to stay outside, and they entered. They went into the bedroom where he was sleeping. The policeman asked me to go back to the neighbours, whilst they talked to him. One of the police officers woke him, but apparently, because he refused to answer questions and cooperate, they tried to arrest him, but he refused to go with them. Eventually, he was escorted to the police car, refusing to get dressed, and was marched away in his boots and his underpants. That giant of a man looked like a downtrodden fool, as I watched him from the neighbour's window, being marched to the police car by two of Her Majesty's Police Officers.

Thank goodness they'd taken him away. I could finally breathe a sigh of relief. As I sat in the chair, I felt numb. My body had gone into shutdown to try and protect me from the emotional trauma that I had just experienced. I thanked the elderly couple and returned to the flat to wait for the police officer to ring me with an update.

A little while later, the policeman got in touch. He asked me if there was anywhere that I could go that was safe. I said that I could go to my mums, who was away on holiday for the Bank Holiday weekend. But my boyfriend had hidden my keys, and my mum's key was on the missing key ring.

The policeman said that he'd call me back after he'd spoken to him.

The policeman called again and said, 'He's hidden the keys in the battery compartment of your ghetto blaster. Gather some valuables together and I'll come and get you in 20 minutes and take you to your mum's house.'

I scrambled around the flat, picking up anything and everything that I thought I might need to keep me going over the next few weeks. I'd no idea whether I would ever return to my little flat. I had a big suitcase for my clothes. My passport and cards and photographs. And weirdly a beautiful new vase that I'd recently bought. In my mind I thought he'd return and try to smash anything that he could, to make my life as miserable as possible, so anything that was easy to break, I took with me. The policeman arrived as promised, and we bundled everything into the police car. I remember him laughing slightly at the picture of me carrying this vase under my arm. I guess he thought, 'I told her anything of value!'

As I walked through the door of my mum's house, I started shaking and crying, as I'd never cried before. The shock had set in! I couldn't believe that I was still alive. I honestly thought my life was about to end the previous night, and felt so grateful to still be alive.

I grabbed a duvet from Mum's spare bed, curled up on the couch, and tried to get some sleep. But sleep didn't come that night. Eventually, at about 6.30 am, and to try and stop the busy chatter of my brain, I decided to make a cuppa and turn on the radio. Every station was playing somber classical music. I thought it was strange, and tried switching stations, but every single one of them was the same. And then there was the announcement that Princess Diana had been killed in a car crash in Paris.

My heart stopped, the sense of shock that I had felt earlier returned to me, and my stomach felt as though it had turned to stone. All of us will forever remember where we were when we heard the announcement of Princess Diana's death, but for me, the memory is exacerbated by the intense and near-death experience of my own that night.

That police officer was wonderful. My absolute hero. I'll never forget what he did for me that night. He was so caring and kind. He went above and beyond to help me, and for that, I'll be forever grateful.

I was working at the pub, and a couple of weeks later, a man approached me at the bar, and said, 'Hello Frances.' When I looked to see who it was, I realised that it was the police officer that had helped me that night. For a moment I didn't recognise who he was, but the recognition must have shone from my face, as I said, 'Oh it's you! I didn't recognise you with your clothes on!' He laughed and I offered to buy him a drink to say thank you for all his help that night.

The kindness of strangers never ceases to amaze me. If it hadn't been for that police officer and the lovely couple across the hallway, I don't know what would have happened to me on that dreadful night in August 1997.

The reason I share this story is to hopefully, be a beacon of hope to others who are going through similar struggles.

People will ask, 'Why did you put yourself in that situation? And my answer now, knowing what I know, is that I was making decisions about my life and relationships based on what happened to me as a child (from my wounded child story,) and because it was playing out in my subconscious, I had no idea it was there until I started to do the healing work.

Throughout my life, I've moved from one relationship to another, choosing men who were also living out their lives from their wounded child place, so what happens is that you attract the same patterns and experiences into your life, until you learn the lessons and break those patterns.

When you hear people say, "I'm online dating and there are no nice men/women out there.' This is not true, but it's their truth. Because they have blocks in their energy system that are stopping them from attracting healthy relationships into their life.

What was the biggest game changer for me?

Making decisions from a place of lack or low self-worth. Feeling like you're the victim and that you're completely unable to change your life. However, this is actually a choice.

You can choose to live your life differently, and I know it sounds like a cliché, but it starts from within. It's the only way change will become lasting,

'You don't know what you don't know.' That is such a relevant phrase and until I realised what was happening to me, I simply did not recognise the cycle in which I was living my life, As I read this story in the present time, I can see with absolute clarity what I was doing, but when I was right there, in the thick of it, I was looking for someone to love me.

If you're projecting from lack and scarcity, this can have a profound impact, not only on you but on your family and friends and if you work for yourself, on your business too. It's easier said than done, but there are some simple ways that you can tell if someone has 'wounded child' stories you need to address.

They see things in black and white, there's no grey. By this, I mean that it's yes or no, there's no compromise with their lives.

Or, you don't seem to be getting anywhere. You're making the same mistakes repeatedly. Look for the patterns. If you're going round and round in circles with relationships or attracting clients that treat you badly, these are key indicators that you have some personal limiting beliefs playing out beneath the surface. It's linked to your self-worth.

Everything is energy. Everything that we are, everything that we do, reflects what is going on beneath the surface. Later, in the book I share my dating experiences, and how every man I met, was the same energetically. Physically they looked different, but deep down they had low self-worth. Because my self-worth was low, I was attracting the same energetic vibration.

When running my own business, I was constantly looking for the next piece of work. I didn't believe in myself, so was copying other design agencies rather than looking within to see what my special gifts were and being able to offer these to my clients. Constantly looking over my shoulder at the competition and envying their growth. Because of this, I worked extra hard, undercutting my competitors, and making my staff work hard too. My energy was disseminated into the business, which meant that there was no fun for me or my staff. No wonder they didn't stay around for long. The business absorbs your energy.

I cannot emphasise how important it is to clear that stuck energy because the holy grail of blocked energy is a direct reflection on how much money you can earn.

Yes, my businesses grew, and over time, they were successful, but what I found was that the bigger the business, the harder I fell.

It's like The Universe was saying to me, 'Yes my dear, that's all well and good, but you still haven't learned what you were put here to learn, so we are going to teach you some lessons.' Boy were they tough lessons to learn.

Your self-worth reflects your self-worth.

Four years ago, I lost my business. I talk in detail about this later. It was at that point that I discovered Energy Medicine, headed by an amazing woman called Louise Reed in Australia. The programme that I went through with her, made me see that it was about emotions locked inside my energy system because emotions are energy in motion. When they get stuck in your energy system and we don't clear them they create dis-ease.

I came to appreciate that in my early life I had to travel that challenging path, it was part of my destiny to experience the trauma I lived through. Without my early experiences, it would not have been possible for me to understand other peoples' 'wounded child stories' and to be placed in this privileged position of being able to help them to heal.

Every one of my experiences was meant to be, to help me see with absolute clarity what my clients have gone through so that I can help with a deep understanding of who they are and the challenges they face. There is never any judgment from me.

I believe that we make decisions in our lives, based on our level of understanding at that time.

I want to thank every single person that has been part of my journey. I've learned deep lessons and now understand myself at a cellular level. In the past, if someone had hurt me, I would drop into victim mode. For example, 'Why is it always me? Why would they want to hurt me in this way? Why can I never get the break that my peers get?'

When now, I ask myself, 'What lesson is this person here to teach me? Why did I need to experience that thing in my life?'

Everything is energy.

As humans, we are mostly made of water and electricity.

We were created and fine-tuned to pick up on subtle nuances. These skills helped us to survive. But over time, in the fast-paced digital world where we value money and success more than anything else, we have lost the art of listening to our intuition.

When we believe in lack and scarcity, that's what we receive.

When we believe in true abundance and give freely with love, then this is attracted back to us. The more we truly believe this, the more we attract.

This statement connects to 'How we do anything is how we do everything.'

For example, if you're settling in your life, look to see where else you're settling. Because if it's in one area, then it's bound to be in other areas too.

If we stopped to listen to what was going on, we'd have a life full of peace and love, which after all is what we crave most of all.

If you don't address the issue that keeps you stuck and playing small, as a business owner what you believe beneath the surface, will reflect at you. It is important to deep dive into what's going on for you.

If you don't go deep and find the heart of the issue, you'll keep going round and round in circles, and this isn't something that we can easily do alone, we need help and guidance to truly recognise the areas locked deep in our psyche which are preventing us from living our best lives and becoming the best possible version of ourselves.

Business has a funny way of reflecting right back at you on what is going on in your energy system.

I've always had an entrepreneurial brain. I see opportunities and gaps in the market all the time. I get this from my dad. We used to run a business together years ago. My mum and dad gave me the best of both worlds. I got my mum's academic brain and my dad's entrepreneurialism. But even though I had all that, I still seemed to get stuck.

I've run seven different businesses in my career. The biggest benefit was that I gained a huge variety of skills.

I started out running a marketing and copywriting business called Marketing Doctor. I had offices and staff and everything that goes with that, but being single and running your own business can be a very lonely place. I started a little side-line, where I invited women in business together, to meet up once a month and created a mastermind group. I spent the first few months trying lots of different ideas to get the format of the meetings flowing, and then, before Christmas (the timing was beautiful) one of the members said to me, 'You know, you've got this working well now. Have you thought about making it bigger than it is?'

I spent that Christmas thinking about how to grow the business, and by the time we came back to work in January, I had a plan to create 6 more groups.

I called it Bird Board. It was for female business owners or women at board level.

The name was brave because some women had negative connotations about the word Bird, but I loved it. It connected with who I was. I say that my middle name is Brave. The name stood out from the rest of the other female networking businesses out there. They were all some form of women in business, businesswomen, managers, you know the sort of thing.

Over the next two years, Bird Board grew rapidly, and at its peak, there were 150 members, across 15 boards along the M62 corridor in the North of England.

But it grew too quickly and soon, I realised that I was struggling to manage the growth.

Part of the membership was two lunches per year where each member could meet up with the rest of the members across all the boards.

They were great big events, and at the busiest lunch, we had nearly 300 women attending.

In the run-up to that final event, I could see that the new member sign-up wasn't as rapid as it had been.

Some of the members of some of the Boards were not getting the same experience as others. Approximately half the boards were near capacity, and others not so, for lots of different reasons. I recognised the need to change the business model so that everyone had the same experience.

I travelled to America with a friend, a few months prior, on a 4-day business retreat to learn how this woman coach was running her business. The plan, over the next 6 months was to convert the business into a hybrid model, where we met online, and I'd host a monthly face-to-face meeting for all the members.

About 10 days before the Bird Board event, I had a meeting with the manager of events at the hotel where we were going to hold the lunch. I asked her to reduce the number of bookings I'd reserved. I had booked for 150 women and wanted to reduce it to 100. The way in which this event was usually subsidised, was by the visitors who attended because they'd pay for their place. But when I looked at the visitor numbers, we had about ten booked to date. I was starting to panic. We weren't getting the numbers. Usually, the members would have taken a table for guests, etc, but that wasn't the case that year.

I sat on a step outside the hotel and opened my phone. I decided to post a short video in the members' Facebook group, telling them how excited I was to be seeing them in two weeks, and did they have anyone that they'd like to bring along.

Two days later, four people had watched that video.

My wounded child, who felt she had not been heard, sprang to the surface and she wasn't being listened to again.

I started spiralling out of control.

No one is listening to me. I might as well just pack it in.

What is the point? This event is going to cost me thousands of pounds and I just don't have it.

That was the lowest point in my career. That pivotal moment when I saw that only four people had watched the video.

Not only that but I was ill. I was working too hard. I was exhausted.

I was going into a financial meltdown. What was I going to do?

The next day, my accountant rang me for something unrelated.

She said, 'Are you ok?' and I burst into tears. I told her everything and she invited me into her office to look at the numbers.

Now, nearly 5 years later, after my healing, I can see with absolute clarity that it was my wounded child.

What would I do differently?

I'd have put my big girl's pants on and got a couple of interest-free credit cards and paid for it with the cards.

The fallout from not doing it was going to cost me far more than I was going to lose by not hosting the event.

My reputation as a businesswoman was on the line. And your reputation in business is everything. If people don't trust you, then you may as well pack your bags and leave town.

As I drove home that day, my world was falling apart before my very eyes.

I called to see my accountant the next day so that we could go through the details together. After asking me lots of detailed questions, we decided to liquidate the company. She said that I needed to do it professionally and that I couldn't do it on my own.

She called a few people, and a couple of days later, I met someone who helped me to formalise the liquidation of Bird Board.

I was devastated. I felt like I'd lost my baby. All that time and energy, building a beautiful business, and helping all those amazing women. I saw it disintegrate before my eyes in a matter of days.

The next few months were the hardest months of my business life. Because there were so many members of Bird Board, it was very public. The liquidator told me to keep my head down. Come off social media, and they would take care of the creditors.

Never had I felt so low. And to make things worse, I was single again, so was going to be spending Christmas on my own.

But tiny miracles do happen, and about a week before Christmas, I received an email in my inbox, inviting me to an online retreat for women.

One of the women who was delivering part of the retreat was Louise Reed – Energy Shaman. Sitting in my PJs, throughout the whole of Christmas and New Year, I immersed myself fully in this online retreat. It was beautiful.

Examples of businesses, and how they function at an energy level.

When a friend of mine was starting in the world of work, she started working for a company that only ever went after the small business owner. They were a marketing company and were charging for social media management, web hosting, and digital marketing packages. Because they were all small businesses and were mindful of their marketing budget, my friend was constantly working hard to keep everyone happy.

The owner used to take everyone out for a drink on Fridays after work, but I could tell from the information that she shared with me that he wasn't thinking big. For him, it was turnover rather than profit, which meant that the staff were running around in circles trying to please everyone.

She now works for a company with a much larger client base. They have high-end clients which means that the average transaction value is much higher.

She told me after she started working there. 'It's much nicer. We get time to focus on the client and add lots more value because we're not distracted by the constant demands of all the other clients. I love it!'

Can you see how both companies were providing the same service, but the culture of each organisation was different?

Because the owner of her current business has an abundance mindset, they have set their business up in the right way, to attract better quality clients. Then their existing clients will recommend them to others in their tribe because the staff has the luxury of time to do a great job. When you think about what you charge, think about the result that your clients get, because people pay for the results, not the service. If you're starting a business, you may as well set it up to succeed, rather than fail.

Everything is energy so everything you do in life reflects what's going on internally. The sooner you clear it, the better your life will become.

The way you do anything is the way you do everything.

When you run a business, it seems to compound the effect of what's going on for you beneath the surface, because your bank account reflects what your self-worth is.

We are so much more than what appears on the surface.

When you're out business networking, the words that come out of your mouth are only a tiny percentage of what people connect with and remember you by. They can sense if you're selling from a place of lack and scarcity. How this plays out may be that your prices are too low. Perhaps you're 'giving away your uterus' to get the next new client. And they will, at some level think, 'That's far too cheap, what's the catch?' How will I possibly get good service, paying that sort of price? Or worse still, 'Do I trust this person to deliver what they say they'll deliver?' The people that do sign up for your services will be the ones who want their pound of flesh and how can you give great service to a client who wants everything for nothing?

In marketing, there's a saying which is 'confusion says no.'

If it doesn't feel congruent, they'll walk away and buy from someone who does feel right.

What happens is we absorb information in our conscious brains at 32 bits per second and in our subconscious minds at 2 million bits per second, so there's so much more beneath the surface than we are aware of.

Our energetic field goes out about 20 feet from our physical body. We feel and sense the world from this sphere. We have five brains.

Our head, our heart, our gut, and two further etheric brains. Like in the ether.

Do you know that sense of someone looking at you when they are standing behind you? That's your etheric brains at work. Almost like your sixth sense.

People talk about gut instinct, but this is not the right brain to listen to. Our gut brain is the one connected to our ego. It protects us and is based on previous experiences. For example, 'I did that before and it didn't work, so I'm not doing that again.'

Your head is the logical brain, of course, but the most powerful brain is your heart.

When you connect to your heart and act from a place of love and an aligned feeling of happiness and fulfilment, this is where the magic starts to happen.

Ask yourself, 'What makes me feel good?' The answer to this question is always the best course of action to take.

Let me explain this in detail, to help you understand it.

Think about all the different energy levels:

If even one of these is out of kilter, then you'll have a discord, have something out of kilter.

SPIRITUAL

Do you trust that everything is happening for a reason? Do you practise what you preach and do you meditate daily, knowing that you're on the right path?

And that if it doesn't work out the way that you planned, there is a lesson to learn for you.

Do you practice gratitude every day? Even for the small things in life?

MENTAL

If you say, 'I believe in the law of attraction,' and yet you're not prepared to put yourself out for someone, then guess what? That's not aligned.

If you ask clients for testimonials, but you're not prepared to give them yourself, that's not aligned.

If you charge high prices, and yet you'll only pay small prices, or want everything for free, that's not aligned.

Look in your bank account. – What is it reflecting at you? Abundance or lack of?

PHYSICAL

What about your health?

How's that doing? Are you fit and healthy? Do you treat your body like a temple or is it wine every night to try and chill out because you're stressed and trying hard to make a success of your business?

Are you 'too busy' to get to that yoga/fitness class?

Are you grabbing fast food when deep down you know your diet needs work?

EMOTIONAL

Look at your relationships. What do they reflect at you?

Love, trust, connectivity, loyalty? Or something else?

In the next chapter, I'm going to share with you what happened to me, to finally make me stand up and listen.

CHAPTER TWO

Everything happens for a reason

In the lead-up to the last Bird Board lunch that we held, I was seeing a guy who had two dogs, one of them was a large Rottweiler called Buster.

One Saturday afternoon, we decided to go to the coast to take them for a run.

As we arrived, the first dog wasn't good at travelling and had been car sick. My chap was cleaning the blanket that she lay on and asked me if I'd hold Buster whilst he sorted her out.

Buster decided to make a run for it. He set off with great gusto and headed straight for the beach. For those of you that know Sands End in the North East of England, it has a large concrete embankment with huge steps that go down onto the sand. I guess they're there to stop the coast from eroding into the sea. With my hand caught in the strap of the lead, Buster took me straight down those concrete steps. I bounced down every step and landed on the sand, and my shoulder was killing me from trying to hold on to the lead and being dragged.

I remember two young guys standing with bottles of water, watching everything unfold. One said, 'We should call an ambulance.'

He could see that my shoulder was hanging much further down than it should. All I could feel was the searing pain. I couldn't walk either, so something was going on in my hip too, but my shoulder was far more painful at the time.

The ambulance arrived. Two women paramedics were brilliant. She took my blood pressure and told me that they needed to wait until it had gone down before she could give me morphine.

Minutes passed and finally, the paramedics were able to administer the drug. I remember the feeling as that morphine hit my body. It was total bliss. The pain just disappeared.

Then they had the challenge of getting me off the beach. The ambulance driver called the RNLI. They arrived with a Land Rover and trailer. It took six of them to lift me with a stretcher and lay me out on the trailer and drive me up the ramp that they used to get the boats into the sea.

At some weird point, there was even a French guy on a jet ski who arrived too. It was like something out of Bay Watch!

My chap stood watching on as the health professionals did their job. He was busy holding onto the dogs, asking me if he could do anything for me. He was distraught at the thought of one of his beloved animals causing me so much pain.

The ambulance crew drove me to A&E and by this time it was about 7 pm on a Saturday, otherwise known as happy hour.

The rooms were filling up, and eventually, I was led to the X-Ray room. We decided that it was probably going to be a long night, so my chap decided to take the dogs home. They'd been locked up in the car, in the hospital car park for a couple of hours. He told me that he would drive straight back. After examining the X-Ray, the male nurse told me that my collarbone was broken, but there was nothing they could do. He strapped it up and told me that I could go home.

I couldn't walk, so they wheeled me out of the hospital in absolute agony. I sat in my wheelchair, waiting for my chap to return so that he could take me home. They didn't set it. They simply strapped me up and sent me on my way.

When I booked into my local GP's the following week, she was horrified that they hadn't even set the bone. Luckily, I had medical insurance, so I booked in with a specialist at the local Aspire Hospital and had my collarbone fixed within a couple of days. I still have a titanium plate there to this day. But as I returned to see the specialist 6 weeks later, I was still struggling to walk. He told me that they didn't have specialist equipment at the private hospital for X Rays of my hip, because usually this type of big break is caused because of a road accident. He said I shouldn't still be limping, so he made a couple of calls across the road at Leeds General Infirmary and asked me to go and see his colleague who specialised in big bone breaks.

I had an MRI scan with this doctor who told me that I'd fractured my hip in 5 places. I was very lucky that I hadn't broken my hip. No wonder walking was so painful!

What I know now is that The Universe was trying to tell me that I was going too fast. That I was on the wrong road. I had to stop.

To make things worse, ten days later I had to host the summer lunch at The Queen's Hotel in Leeds in front of 250 women. I couldn't function. I couldn't get up the stairs, I couldn't drive, and I couldn't dress, so I moved in with my mum. She had to shower me, dress me, and drive me there. We stayed until I delivered my speech, and I was home in bed by teatime.

Secondary Gain Stories

Let's discuss something common such as excess weight.

When someone is overweight, their logical mind knows that they need to exercise more and eat less. She is doing all those things, but the weight is still not shifting.

The excess fat is creating an extra layer of comfort between her and her external world. Because there is an imprisoned emotion or a feeling of isolation that she doesn't want to see.

She wants love, and the way that she feeds herself love is the way that her mother taught her as a child, by giving her treats. They don't call it comfort food for nothing. When we're feeling down, we don't pick up a carrot or celery stick, it's always something that is not a healthy choice. She's eating to fill an inner void.

These are what we call secondary gain stories. There's something beneath the surface that her subconscious is benefiting from, that her conscious mind knows is completely illogical.

Those comforts can be food, but they can also be drugs, alcohol, sex, or gambling to name but a few.

If blocked energy isn't cleared within 3 – 6 months, it becomes stuck in our energy system, and this can cause dis-ease.

Let me share an example of this for you so that you see what I mean.

One of the things that happened to me was that I kept having these strange attacks on my body where I could not breathe. I would pass out on the floor, and come around, after an hour or two. Afterward, they completely drained me. I needed to go to bed to sleep off the effects of the attacks. It felt like I was having a heart attack after each episode. After a week in the hospital and lots of investigations, they found a gallstone, the size of a Cadbury's Cream Egg sitting in my chest where my ribs touch, right in my heart centre. I had the gallstone and my gallbladder removed and the surgeon said that he had never seen a gallstone as big as mine.

Gallstones represent bitterness and anger, that was still held in my energy system.

Gall stones are made of calculi, which is an expression of a hardened life. I was being told to free myself of the past and allow myself to manifest true love.

I wasn't listening to what my body was telling me. When you don't listen, your guides will send you stronger and stronger messages until you do listen.

Energetically, our bodies tell us everything we need to know about our lives.

When I think about these things, they make sense. A powerful Shaman told me that my collarbone was where my wings were attached. I'd broken my wing, so how was I meant to head a business called Bird Board without my wings? And fracturing my hip bone signified inflexibility. That I no longer want to move. I was stuck with this business, and I didn't know how to move forward.

It was my left side too. My feminine energy. I'd lost touch with my intuitive self, the creative self. My sense of who I was.

I found myself driving from one Bird Board meeting to another with no time to breathe in between the meetings.

I was being told to slow down, even by some of the members, but I wasn't listening.

In the next chapter, I'll show you where I was going wrong, and how learning to listen to your inner voice is the key to your unfolding. Plus, the absolute main reason why it's best to follow your heart.

CHAPTER THREE

Learning to listen to your inner voice and not someone else's opinions

When you have a lack of self-worth, you tend to check in with other people all the time.

Asking people's opinions can be very self-destructive.

I see women in Facebook Groups asking for opinions about a new brand or photograph for their website. What tends to happen is that they'll get a whole raft of opinions.

The problem is that most of the women in the group are not their target audience. They're not a branding consultant, or remotely qualified from a marketing perspective to give this advice. The person that asked, is no further forward.

The worst thing you can do is ask your family. Unless of course, they've earned a living in that area of expertise.

The reason for this is that they come at this from a completely different perspective than you.

They want to keep you safe. They still think of you as their little girl, so they'll probably say things to you like, "I do wish you just get a proper job!"

That was my mum by the way. She had worked for the council all her life and took early retirement at 55, with her government pension.

Now don't get me wrong, if that's for you, then good for you. But it wasn't for me. I felt like I'd sold my soul to the devil by working for someone else. Believe me, I've tried it on a few occasions, and a few months in, I think, 'What the hell am I doing?'

Do what you love, and you'll never work a day in your life. There has never been a truer word said. Because when you do what you love, you'll be passionate about becoming an expert in that field. You'll go the extra mile for your clients.

But most of all, you'll make an amazing role model for your children. They'll see a woman who loves her work. Who comes home from work, full of love and passion, that she shares with her family. And who, as a child doesn't want that?

I have a neighbour, who has a great big high-flying job. She used to commute to Liverpool every day for her job From Halifax! That's about 1.5 hours each way. She used to leave every morning slamming the door on the way out so that the whole street could hear her.

She has two children, and those two kids used to get the wrath of her tongue every night. I know because I could hear her screaming at them. Those poor children. I heard her scream at her husband one afternoon, 'It's me that pays for everything in this house!' If ever there was a couple that needed to look in the mirror at what they were doing to their children, it is them. It's all about the money for them, but what I saw was a very unhappy family.

Coming up in the next chapter, I'll share some examples of how negative language can shape your beliefs.

CHAPTER FOUR

See how The Universe reflects at you what you're thinking

Your life is the choice of all the decisions that you've made so far. Because you are what you think about most of the time.

Language has energy. The way we think about things tends to come straight out of our mouths when we least expect it.

The best example of this is when you are stressed and have had a bad day, the stuff that your parents used to say to you when you were little, you find yourself saying to your children.

It can be so destructive, and it's also your negative self-talk. Things like:

> Who do you think you are?
>
> Don't be so big-headed.
>
> Don't be so clever.

I can hear all those comments right now as a small child. It's not your parents' fault. They were doing the best they could with the tools that they had. It's learned behaviour, to keep us playing small. To keep us in our little box and be the worker bees for the more successful business owners. If we think back to how life used to be 100 or 200 years ago. The healthy, successful mill owners (here in the North) needed us to farm the fields and work the mills for their precious textile mills, etc.

It didn't pay for them to encourage us to be the best version of ourselves, because we'd want to be in charge.

But things are different now. We can have anything we want. We have the world at our fingertips. We are so blessed to live in the Western world, with most of us having modern technology to connect to the internet. If you have a phone and the internet, you can create anything your heart desires.

For example, I know someone who always negatively thinks about things.

I used to date him. He'd say things like, "I know you're going to dump me.' I don't think I'm enough for you.' And guess what? We're not together anymore. He manifested his beliefs.

He's a nice guy. But I started to believe his beliefs and his neediness was not attractive quality that I wanted in my life. I wanted an equal. Someone to hold my hand and stand by my side, not someone who needed constant reassurance that he was good enough. I've had enough of that in my life.

As I write this, I find it interesting that my philosophy on finding a man has changed. I used to think that there were no nice men out there. That men didn't like successful women. What a load of rubbish!

It can be tricky to catch your negative self-talk. Because usually, it's buried beneath the surface, and when you're intelligent, the negative self-talk is even more challenging to find.

I have a bucket on my desk, to help capture them. When I hear myself thinking or saying something less than optimal, I write it on a Post-It Note and put it in my Limiting Belief bucket.

Then, when I have a little reflection time, I'll pull those sticky notes out. Look to see if there are any themes and turn the note over and replace it with a more empowering belief. Because I'm clairsentient, I feel into the energy of those written words, does it feel empowering?

Does it feel aligned to who I am becoming? If the answer is yes, then the words are aligned.

I've created a 5-minute mantra that I read out to myself every morning and evening.

To help you I'll share it below:

> *I will earn £X,000 per month by the end of 2023 and £XXX,000 by the end of 2024.*

By doing the work that I love because I am the spiritual one and I see the uniqueness of everyone.

I have created a business that helps women to be financially independent by running their successful businesses. I connect them; I see synergies and opportunities so that they flourish and grow. I'm sharing my knowledge to help them develop a smart business with a blend of real and energy world skills to help them become amazing business leaders.

I will have developed a perfect programme by listening to my guides and my intuition and meditating to take aligned action.

Your subconscious doesn't know the difference between real and imagined. The sooner you start to reprogramme your subconscious, the better off you'll be.

Women have a hard time with their self-worth. It comes up often in our healing sessions.

They'll say things like, I don't think I can do that thing. And it's because of the programming in our energy systems. We've been taught to play small and be subservient for most of our lifetimes and that belief is buried deep within our subconscious. Let's get that out once and for all.

It makes me feel angry!

I want to shout from the rooftops. It's not your fault. You've been programmed.

Just because you've had a couple of knocks in life, doesn't mean that you're not able to do that thing that you set out to do. Keep going. You're learning as you go.

You'll be brilliant at it.

When you take things out to market, it's like waves on the shore. You take your product out, and then it comes back, you need to tweak and change it and then take it out again.

I don't think any product of mine was ever perfect the first time around, I kept changing and adapting it.

When I launched Bird Board, it took a few months to get the format right.

I kept asking for feedback from the women on the board, until eventually, we got it right. We may have an amazing idea, but we must take it to market and test it first, to see whether there's a demand for it.

TASK

Look at your bank account, your home, and your relationships – journal what they're reflecting on you.

Does your bank account show a healthy balance that's steady all the time?

Or does it ebb and flow like the tide and at the end, is there too much month and not enough money?

Are your relationships volatile? Do you love your family and friends, and do you see them regularly, or do you have a stop, start a relationship with them?

What about your love life? How is that looking?

Does your partner empower you? Do they bring out the best in you? Or do they belittle you and make you feel small?

Beliefs destroy and bliefs create. What powerful stories do you tell yourself, that your subconscious believes?

What are your empowering beliefs?

What are the common themes between them all?

When I did this exercise for the first time, I could see, that if every area of my life was loved, including myself, they would be magnificent.

If I focused and decided, and went all in, it could be amazing.

When I got to a certain level, I pulled away.

I couldn't move forward and grow because of a lack of consistency.

It was all about my lack of self-worth. I was sabotaging my growth because I didn't feel worthy of success.

Where it all began

As children, we learn all our beliefs and actions from our primary caregivers, (usually our parents,) so no matter how much inner work you do, you still don't know, what you don't know, and this is how energy work helps.

My mum was 17 when she had me, she was a child herself. My parents stayed together but had nothing, so it was a tough upbringing. She told me that she got pregnant to get away from her dad.

Grandad was a proud Yorkshireman, with lots of brothers. They were expected to pitch in and help around the house. He was a typical alpha male who did not talk about his feelings. And brought his children up that way. He didn't speak to my mum until I was three months old because of the shame her pregnancy brought to the family. My Grandma was a beautiful woman. She was so kind and thoughtful. She was 12 when her mum died, so had no role model to show her how to be a mum, but she did it so well. When my grandma died, we lost the glue that connected our family.

Mum and Dad were still busy growing up, yet they went on to have another daughter. My sister and I learned how to grow up fast.

They taught us to be strong and resilient. They taught us independence and being able to stand up for ourselves. But the thing that we lacked was unconditional love, and as you read the following stories, you'll see how that manifested in my adult life.

I was always the sensitive one. The one that would burst into tears if I got told off as a child. My dad used to say, 'I only needed to look at you and you would cry.'

I believe that as children, we choose our parents because of the lessons they must teach us. All the anger and blame I had for my parents when I was younger is gone. My learning has taught me that they were doing the best that they could with the skills that they'd learned from their parents, and their parent's parents. And let's not forget, that they had wounded child stories too.

Mum was expected to look after her two younger sisters, whilst her parents worked hard. And Dad. His life was really challenging. He told me stories of going to school with a jam sandwich for his lunch and not having sixpence to go to a friends' birthday party with, so he didn't go.

My Harry Potter Scar

My lack of self-worth had dominated my life because of the belief in my subconscious energy system around not knowing unconditional love.

In its purest form, we should all know unconditional love. That we are loved, even though we make mistakes, and get grumpy.

I felt like I did not know that feeling. I knew that my parents loved me, but not unconditionally. I felt that there were always conditions attached.

I recognised, whilst working with a healer, that I was born with healing powers. An intuitive knowing that I can heal people, but what she helped me discover, is that I struggled because of the life that I lived as a small girl.

During my journey into rediscovering my healing powers, a fabulous healer called Joy Fisher, asked me if I'd be happy to do a remote healing session. She wanted to practise it over Zoom with me, to see if she could feel the energetic powers remotely. She encouraged me to lie flat on the floor as she sent healing energies through my body. As the session started, I could feel my body start to move, and jerk. A little like small electric jolts running through my energy system. We worked from the top to the bottom of my body. As she reached the top of my head she said, 'Did you bump your head when you were little, do you have a scar on your forehead?' I said, 'Yes!' When I was about two, I fell down some concrete steps, and a piece of stone lodged in my forehead. I was busy watching some little girls play with dolls and their prams when I fell. Mum told me to get up, and as I stood up, she saw a stone. There was no blood, but she was scared of taking the stone out, in case she couldn't stop the bleeding, and took me by bus to A&E. To this day I have a tiny scar, right in the middle of my forehead.

Joy told me that this was my Harry Potter scar. It was where my gift was held, I was so unable to cope with what was happening in my life when I was small, that I closed my third eye chakra down. I stopped being able to see energetically.

She said, 'Do you want me to open it up again for you?'

'Yes, absolutely, bring it on,' I replied. What is interesting since that time, is that when I started my healing practice, I felt my healing energy in my shoulder blades. I call them my angel wings. Healing energy is like a muscle, when you use it, it becomes stronger and stronger. Since that eventful day, my whole body can feel the healing energy.

Clairvoyants are the ones that are more commonly known. They see things. But I'm clairsentient, which means that I feel the energy. When I'm given a message that I need to explore, or I'm being told that we are on the right path, the hairs on my body stand on end, like little electrical currents shooting up and down the back of my body.

My mum and dad were so broke when they first married, that a man came to the door, buying hair for wigs, and when I was around two, my mum sold my beautiful golden wavy hair to that man.

When I see the two photographs of me. One before I had my hair cut and the accident, and the other at my mum's best friend's wedding about 12 months later. I don't recognise myself. I'm like a different child. Something deep within me had shifted. And it has taken over 50 years to get that little girl back.

I'm around 18 months old, just before the accident happened.

This picture is at my mum's best friend's wedding as her Bridesmaid, after I'd had my hair cut off. Can you see the large ball of light down in the right-hand corner? I believe that this is my spirit guide. Protecting me, looking after me.

CHAPTER FIVE

Masculine and Feminine Energy

Based on the theory that everything is energy. Masculine and feminine energy run through our bodies, so your body has masculine and feminine sides. The Chinese describe it as yin and yang. Masculine energy is the action taking you. The part of you that makes things happen, and feminine energy is the intuitive, creative self. Where do all those wonderful ideas come from, that make you, your unique self?

We all have these qualities within our energy system, but sometimes they can be less than optimal.

Imagine the energy that it takes to write a book. You need to have feminine energy to be creative and write it. Then you step into your masculine energy to market and sell it. And to run a business we need both.

Sometimes we come across beautiful couples, who we know have a great relationship.

He adores her. He would do anything to please her because she sits in her powerful feminine energy.

They are total equals in every way but admire each other's qualities. He connects to his masculine and provides everything that she needs to be powerful. She loves him with all her heart and would do anything for him too. And together they make a beautiful union. You know that the sex will be amazing because they trust and respect one another. You know that together they've created something magical, and they're invincible. It's them against the world.

The perfect example of this is in the film, A Star is Born. When Bradley Cooper first sees Lady Gaga at the beginning of the film, she is singing in a local bar, and he is smitten with her. He already knows that she is the one. He encourages her. He seeks her out and makes her step outside of her comfort zone because he knows that she has a beautiful gift to share with the world, but Lady Gaga is lacking in her self-worth. Little by little he encourages her to shine her light for all to see but to the detriment of his career. (Distorted masculine energy).

It's one of my all-time favourite films. And told so beautifully.

When I worked for my dad years ago, he would always pay me in pound notes. I remember that feeling, making me feel like I had to be humble and grateful for the payment. Almost asking me to hold out my hand for the payment, as he counted it out into my hand.

It was the same with my ex-husband. He insisted that I pay him cash for the maintenance. Partly because he didn't want it going into his account and partly as a control thing.

> Where does money control you?

> Are you having to work hard to make money?

> Do you always feel like there is only just enough?

If you feel like this about money, then guess what? You'll feel like this about men too.

I urge you to do the inner work and release those limiting beliefs that are keeping you from playing small. You deserve so much more than that.

TASK

I'd like you to get out your journal and write about what you recognise as your optimal masculine and feminine.

Optimal feminine energy may be:

- You Love to receive
- You empower others to step into their optimal.
- You surrender to The Universe.

Less than optimal may be:

- You look for external validation
- You have weak personal boundaries
- You need someone else in your life to feel whole.

Optimal masculine energy may be:

- You love to give

- You take responsibility for all your actions

- You are brave in the face of challenge and change.

Less than optimal may be:

- You may be abusive toward yourself or other people

- There is always drama

- A need for power and control.

Explore your optimal and distorted energy.

CHAPTER SIX

Money is masculine energy

The way that most of us were taught about money has been passed down from one generation to another, from either abundance or lack and scarcity. The way that you think about money is the way you think about men.

Money is masculine energy. I know that sounds a little strange but think about it. Money is a provider. It gives you the things that you want in your life. It must be masculine right?

Now more than ever money is becoming less tangible. It is a man-made thing that man created centuries ago to make the bartering system easier.

You weren't going to be able to simply swap two chickens for a cow, so they created money to make it a fairer system. But then in 1933, governments created the global system and taxes were introduced, and the whole thing became so messy, it's difficult to see what it was put there for in the first place.

They swapped money of substance (gold) for money of form (paper notes) and the money of form, isn't worth anything. We are simply programmed to believe that it is.

The greed and corruption undertaken in this world for money is off the scale.

What if we stripped it back? Supposing we stop to imagine what money can create and solve.

Money is a beautiful thing.

It doesn't change who you are when in possession of it. It reinforces who you are. Fundamentally if you're a good person, money allows you to help more people.

If you have any negative beliefs around money, such as:

Rich people are bad.

All money does is create greed and sadness.

I urge you to look at those beliefs and get rid of them as quickly as you can, because if that's your belief system about money, then you'll never become successful.

TASK

Let's deep dive into some of those beliefs.

Give yourself a score out of ten for the following two statements. Zero is that it isn't important at all, and 10 is that it is very important.

1. How important is money to me?
2. Money is one of the most important things in my life.

If the second answer is a lesser number, then you have some work to do.

Money should be important to you. It helps you be a bigger, better version of yourself and what you stand for.

What's your emotional belief around money?

There is never enough money.

There's always just enough money.

There is enough money.

There is always lots of money.

If I am successful, people won't like me.

I do/don't need a man to be successful.

To help you, here are some examples of distorted energy that came up for me.

See if any of them resonate with you.

Good men are scarce.

I am envious of those who have great relationships with men or money.

I don't feel valued – I attract men who don't value me.

I don't like it when men/money have a hold over me.

Money is the master, and I am the slave.

How do money/men hold power over you?

In what relationships are you the slave?

Next, I'd like you to take pen to paper and journal. Ask yourself these questions:

Why is money not important to me?

Money gives you more of what you need to improve your success.

Money doesn't make you happy, it simply gives you more of the things that you want to make your life more pleasurable,

To make you the best version of yourself, or market yourself.

It increases your vibration.

Money is a beautiful thing, there is nothing negative about money.

The next thing I'd like you to do is:

Download The Secret App

This is because money doesn't care whether it's real or pretend.

I love this app. It's the first one I paid for. At the time I wrote this book, it was about £4.50 and I thought, 'My words, paying for an app, I must be crazy.' But I love it, and it's worth every penny.

Every day you receive a cheque to spend, and as you spend it, the cheque increases. You can go wild with this and once you've bought everything that you need, start to create good in the world, by creating a charity or gifting it to your friends and family.

There's a gratitude section where you list everything, you're grateful for.

A giving section, where you track everything that you've gifted to people and daily inspirations.

It is beautiful. You get daily affirmations about money, and there's space to collect the manifested money. Give it a try.

There can be lots of negative connotations connected with money.

For example Filthy rich – even that feels negative.

Are there any similarities between the way that you think about men and money?

Similarities may be:

- Good men are scarce. They're all taken.
- I can't be successful without a man.
- I need a man to take care of me.

How do you work on the positive?

The best way I've found to work on yourself, and your belief system is to create positive affirmations.

Now I don't mean simply saying something to yourself in a mirror every day.

You absolutely must believe them.

Once you've discovered what these negative beliefs are, I'd like you to write them down on a Post-It note, then on the reverse write a positive statement.

For example:

I must work hard for a living can become…

- I work in a smart way so that money comes to me effortlessly.

- I will always be provided for abundantly.

- Having wealth helps me to lead and empower in a smarter way.

The next step is to add more detail by saying how you're going to do this.

Here's one that I created to give you an example.

I earn £10,000 per month by doing the work that I love. I help women on the inside and outside, to be financially independent by releasing energetic blocks that stop them from stepping into their true potential. I show them how to manage their successful business from their powerful feminine. With residual income and connecting to their WHY.

Money needs direction and clarity. You're in charge of the money, not the other way around. If you run your own business, set up a standing order every month and pay yourself first. There is positive energy to this action. You are saying to The Universe that you value yourself and the work that you do.

If you find this a little difficult to get your head around try, for the first month, a smaller amount and every month increase it. What happens is that energetically you are setting up an expectation to get paid for the hard work that you do.

The Universe knows no different, it will find a way to pay you.

I promise it's absolute genius. Try it. Set up a standing order next month to pay yourself £100 and give it a title. Call it MONTHLY SALARY so that you know it is expected every month. Please let me know how you get on and increase it by £50 every month.

Now a little disclaimer. You must do the work, and we'll come onto that in more detail further down the line. You must meet The Universe halfway and go out and get the work done. You cannot simply sit there and manifest it. It doesn't work like that.

Money loves responsibility

I'm asking you to start to take responsibility for your money.

By making sure you're opening your credit card statements every month. Knowing what you need to set aside each month to pay your bills. Saving some for emergencies too.

The next thing I'd like you to do is write a letter to money to explore your relationship with it.

Imagine that you'd won £10,000,000 on the lottery. What would you do differently?

Isn't it funny that sometimes we feel we don't deserve success and that within a few years, some people have spent every single penny? It's like its dirty money and they must get rid of it quickly.

It's because they are vibrating at scarcity and lack. Or on a more subtle level, they don't feel that their self-worth is great enough. That they are not worthy of success.

And finally, on the subject of money, remember that I said The Universe doesn't know whether it's real or fake?

Demonstrate that you have plenty.

It doesn't need to be lots of money. It could be small acts of kindness. By putting one-pound coins in trolleys at the supermarket, for people to find.

Why not invite friends for dinner?

Or send someone a thank you card through the post.

I was in the supermarket a little while ago, and I bought my weekly shop. As the girl at the check-out was ringing up the items, I realised that I'd forgotten my purse. I was mortified. A lady was standing behind me who said, 'How much is it? I'll pay for that. You can pay me when you get home.' She had no idea who I was, and I was stunned that a stranger would trust me to pay for my shopping. Even the girl at the checkout was speechless.

At the time it was about £40. I spoke to her in the car park and took her email address and bank details and said that I'd return the money straight away and that I'd like to gift her an energy healing session for being so kind.

She told me that she was a consultant and believed in energy work. I sent her my details, but she never did take me up on the treatment.

Isn't that a beautiful example of the kindness of strangers?

The Universe has a wonderful way of paying you back for all these random acts of kindness that you give to others.

In the next chapter, I'm going deep. The reason I share these personal stories is not for self-pity, or "poor me" syndrome, it's to help you see what I couldn't see for such a long time.

The patterns in my destructive relationships.

I wish someone had sat me down years ago, to shine a mirror in my face and gently, with love, show me where I was going wrong. I hope that reading this book, may help you or someone you love so that they don't have to go through similar experiences.

CHAPTER SEVEN

Self worth and my dating experiences

My first serious boyfriend

I met him just before my 16th birthday. He was three years older than me, so it felt like I'd got a catch with my older boyfriend.

My sister and I spent our evenings in the local park. A girl approached me one evening and said, "That boy over there fancies you and wants to know if you'll go out with him."

I could feel myself going red, I looked over to check him out. He was handsome. The typical, tall dark, and handsome. He seemed much older because all the boys at school were small, and just hitting puberty. But he was about 3 and a half years older than me, so he appeared to me to be so grown up. I said yes!

We chatted for a while and over the weeks, got to know each other a little bit more.

I used to babysit on a Friday night for a neighbour who lived down the road from me.

The new boyfriend would come and visit on his way home from the pub at about 10 o'clock. I thought he was wonderful. He was smart, and into music, and I used to walk up the road to meet him from work every night.

I was a very naive 16-year-old.

What I know now is that he was just like his father. An Irish drunk, who would blow his weekly wage on the day that he got paid, on drink and gambling, and his poor mum, who worked part-time as a cleaner, would have to find the money to support her three boys on her part-time earnings.

His mum was a Londoner, and he was confused about who he was. He supported the IRA and West Ham United. A real blend of the two cultures.

He was very aggressive when he'd been drinking. Just like his dad, who beat his mum when he had lost his money in the Bookies or had been drinking too much.

When I first met him, I worked full time as an office junior but decided after about a year that I wanted to go to college to do an art course.

I loved it! It opened my eyes to what my world could be like. I met new and interesting friends. This new confidence started to seep into our relationship, with varied passions and interests, and he did not like it. I was growing up and learning to be independent with my own views and opinions, he was losing control of me.

I also worked in the local pub (at age 17.)

I'd been going to this pub for about 6 months and the landlady asked me if I wanted a job. The extra income was a bonus because being a poor art student, I wasn't earning any money at that time.

The landlady didn't ask me for ID when I started, and I got paid in cash, so it was to her surprise that I celebrated my 18th birthday in the pub that year. Our relationship was starting to crumble. I called a halt to it after two years and he did not like it. About two months after we had split up, I decided to go into town and meet my friends from college one Saturday night for a girl's night out. I caught the bus into town and went upstairs onto the top deck.

He was sitting at the back of the bus. My heart was pounding. He never went into town, so I knew that he was looking for me.

I tried to keep out of his way and sat at the front. He walked right up to me and sat next to me. My mouth was dry. My heart pounding and I had no idea what was coming next.

He asked me again why I had finished with him. We'd been through this on numerous occasions, and I could smell the alcohol, on his breath.

He was probing me about whether I'd met anyone else and whether I was out on the town with my friends, looking for a new man.

As I got off the bus, he grabbed my arm and started dragging me in the opposite direction to where I was meeting my friends. They were at the opposite end of the high street. I fought with every ounce of energy, but he knocked me to the floor and dragged me by my hair through the street in the opposite direction to where I was meeting my friends. People were watching, as he laced into me. Hitting and shouting at me. Calling me terrible names. He twisted my arm up my back and punched me in the face.

The next thing I knew was that he had grabbed my handbag. He rifled through it, took my purse, and ran off with it.

I was crying and trembling and didn't know what to do next. I had no money so didn't even have the bus fare to get home.

I walked down the street in shame, with blood trickling down my face to go and meet my friends. Perhaps, at least they'd be able to give me my bus fare to get home.

I saw the look of horror on their faces as they saw me walking toward them. As I explained what had happened, my friend said that there was no way that I was going home. They would all chip in and lend me some money. I protested, but they would hear nothing of it. They took me into the local pub toilets and helped me get cleaned up. Luckily, I hadn't broken anything.

We had been out for about 2 hours, and I spotted him in one of the local bars.

He was getting drunk on my money!

I was furious and walked right up to him and asked him for my purse back. He gave it to me, but of course, there was nothing in it.

I saw him recently standing outside a Wetherspoons pub at 10 am on a Monday with no front teeth. He smiled at me, and I looked away and thought, 'Did I date that man? What was I thinking? I must have been crazy!'

The big bag of letters

When I met my firstborn's father, I was 19. We were going into town at the weekends. He was a guy who was in the group of friends that we went out with.

I fancied him, and over the weeks, we started to see one another.

I was working as a temp at The Halifax Bank, and we'd only been going out for about 3 months when a thought struck me. 'I haven't had a period for a while, it should be due by now?'

I mentioned it to the girls I worked with, and they urged me to get a pregnancy test, just to make sure.

Pregnancy test kits weren't sold so easily back then, so I made an appointment at the Laura Mitchell Clinic (a local women's health centre) and the result came back, not negative, or positive. I was told to go back first thing the following morning with an early morning sample, and they would re-do the test. I returned the following day and to my absolute surprise, the test was positive. Not only that, but I was 12 weeks pregnant, and I had the weekend to decide whether I wanted to keep the baby or not. The doctor was kind. She had an understanding look in her eyes, as I sat on the chair in her office, trying to absorb what she had just told me.

My head was in a spin. What was I going to do?

How could I tell him? How could I tell my family?

I told him that night, and we spent all weekend talking through options.

On Sunday evening, we were standing at the bus stop waiting to get the last bus home. It was the final decision time, and I said that there was no way that I could end the pregnancy. He was still at university, and I knew, logically that termination was the right thing to do, because we would be repeating the same patterns as my mum and dad. We had no money. It wasn't the right time. We were both so young, but I simply could not terminate the pregnancy.

On Monday morning I went back to the Laura Mitchell Clinic to let them know what I'd decided to do. Keep my baby. That morning everything started to shift and change. My life would never be the same again. As I returned to work, I started to plan the conversations that I needed to have with those close to me. I'd only known him for three months! This was going to be a true test of our relationship. But I knew in my heart of hearts, even if it didn't work out between us that I simply couldn't have a termination.

He wasn't the most communicative of people and kept his feelings and thoughts to himself, and because I was three months pregnant, I was starting to show a little.

I had to tell my mum. I was so nervous, and she took it better than I expected.

I asked her if she would tell Dad because I was too scared to tell him.

When Mum told Dad, we had the inevitable conversation the following day.

Phrases like…

> 'You've made your bed you better lie in it.'
>
> 'I might have expected it of your sister, but not of you!'
>
> 'We are not having another baby in this house.'

When the air had cleared and they'd had a chance to absorb what I'd just shared with them, Dad said, "I'll pay the deposit on a house, and you can get your own place. "

So that was that. I started looking for a house and found a little two-bedroomed terrace at King Cross. It was the princely sum of £10,000 with a £200 deposit.

As I was waiting for the house sale to go through, the baby's dad was still deciding whether he was going to move in with me.

He still hadn't told his mum that I was pregnant!

I was now about 5 months pregnant, and I decided to take the bull by the horns. If he hadn't told his mum by now, he wasn't going to tell her. We went down to his parent's house. His mum was ironing, and he went for a bath. I asked her to sit down because I had something to tell her.

She was flawed and very upset.

Right up until the week that I was moving into my house, I still wasn't sure whether he was going to move in with me. But he did. I think he arrived with two suitcases and his stereo system.

The first few months were hard. There were three of us sleeping in a single bed, me, him, and Bump. I was getting bigger by the day. His mum kindly bought us a double bed. It felt like an absolute luxury. We begged and borrowed lots of second-hand furniture and we were living on my £80 per week wage and his student grant. It was tough!

My beautiful Daniel came along that August, and I had to stop working for a while, so things got even more challenging.

But as with most things, you get through, you manage.

He finished his final year at Huddersfield Poly and got a great job in Yeadon, but we had no car. His dad very kindly, let him use his car to get to work. He would walk down the road to collect it in the mornings and drop it off at teatime.

One day when Daniel was about 18 months old, I had to go looking for something in the top cupboard in the big built-in wardrobe in our bedroom. Right at the back of the cupboard, I came across a carrier bag full of letters.

As I started to read the letters, I could feel myself go cold all over. They were from a girl called Christine, who he had been seeing before me, he'd met her at a student exchange at university, and she was from Germany.

She'd been writing letters to him, at his parents' address, and when he went down to collect the car for work, he'd pick them up.

The theme of every letter was about how much she missed him and loved him and some of them were very intimate.

I knew as I read them, and checked the dates on the envelopes, that she wasn't even aware of me or our boy, and that he had kept us a secret all this time.

I was heartbroken. I could feel our little family falling apart, right there before my eyes. The trust was gone. I could feel my heart beating, breaking, as I waited for him to walk through the door from work. I'd placed the letters in the middle of the lounge floor, waiting for him to return.

The tears of anger and betrayal streamed down my face, I told him that I wanted him to leave and take his letters and his belongings with him.

Our relationship finished as quickly as it had begun.

I was now a single parent with little money, and a nearly 2-year-old to bring up.

My boy was a very quiet, sensitive child. He would sit and play on his own with his toys, such a little sweetheart. I think back now and recognise that I had post-natal depression. Being only 19 when I had him, and having had very little support. I remember the midwife coming to my house about a week after I'd arrived home from hospital with him. I was up to my eyes in nappies and baby stuff, and she said, 'Haven't you got anyone to help you?' I said no. My parents worked and my partner was at Uni. I just got on with it.

I didn't really talk to Daniel. I didn't know how to. It felt weird talking to a baby who couldn't reply. I wasn't taught how to be a mum. None of us are, but I didn't realise how important all that stuff was, which meant that he was a late talker. I guess that is one of the reasons why he feels emotion in the way that he does because it was the way that he could read me, through my emotions. Gosh, that is hard to write.

I started working in a local pub in town. I'd clean in the morning before the pub opened, and then get changed and worked behind the bar. I got a free child place for Daniel at a childminder, just down the road from me. She was brilliant with him. He loved going there and he developed in leaps and bounds by being with other children. I remember having conversations with his dad about paying maintenance and access.

He must have had an agreement with his boss because when he finally filled his forms in, he paid me £16 per month maintenance for years. I remember watching Daniel sit by the window in our first little house, waiting for his daddy to come and collect him on a Saturday afternoon. It broke my heart to see that look of disappointment on his face when his dad didn't come for him.

A single parent working full time.

Daniel was about two. At the time you could work 20 hours a week and still claim Family Allowance. I started working in a pub in Halifax town centre. The landlord and lady were brilliant. They were so supportive of me, and my situation and they loved my boy.

I'd start work at 9 am, I'd clean the pub, and then go upstairs, change my clothes, come down, and work behind the bar. I loved it. It was a way of me getting paid and still having some kind of social life. Sometimes, if they were stuck at weekends, I'd take him with me and put him upstairs in their bed with the baby alarm on.

I made some new friends and met some brilliant people in that pub.

One night, one of the regulars asked me out for a drink. I was to meet him at Brighouse Bus Station. I'd arranged for a babysitter and went all the way there on the bus, and waited for him, for what seemed like an eternity. He didn't show up. I was fuming. But because I'd arranged a babysitter, it seemed silly to go straight home, and because I knew the regulars in the pub and of course the staff behind the bar, I decided to go into the pub, and stand at the other side of the bar for a change and have a drink with my mates.

There were two regulars there whom I sort of recognised, and one of them bought me a drink. Before we knew it, we'd been chatting for about 2 hours, and it was time for me to go home.

He asked me if I'd like to see him again, and I said yes. He was nice. He had kind eyes.

Two and half months on, we'd spent a lovely Christmas together. I lived on my own, so he'd spent most of his time with me and my boy.

One day out of the blue he asked me to marry him!

I was so shocked, I said, I'd need to think about it, but two days later, I said yes.

He looked like he'd be a great provider for us. He had a good future and was conscientious and kind.

In those first few months of our meeting, we had a couple of challenges. One of them was that he was so used to being single, and his doting mum just preparing something for him so that it could be warmed up when he got home.

I'd make the evening meal, and he'd go straight to the pub after work, so some nights it would be 7 pm or after when he walked through the door.

There was no way that I was accepting this behaviour, so one night I left his food in the oven. When he got home, it was as black as coal. He never did it again.

On the 14th of February 1987, we married at St Marks Church, King Cross.

It snowed that day. A friend of my dad's videoed the day, and there's a shot of my sister in the churchyard shivering because she was so cold. My boy was dancing to the organ music as we went into the vestry to sign the register.

We were happy. It felt like my fairy tale was beginning.

Finally, I'd found someone who loved me. Who was faithful and kind and wanted nothing but the best for me and my boy.

We moved from that tiny little two-bedroomed terrace and used the money from the house to buy a bigger house in Queensbury. And after a year of marriage, I was pregnant with child number two.

I remember as he was being born saying 'I love you' as another little soul entered our lives. A beautiful baby boy.

Now as you know if you're a parent, the cracks can start to show when you're both working hard and trying to bring up a family. We were no different from ordinary people. He was working lots of hours, not getting home till 7 pm some nights, and then playing rugby on a Saturday and going to watch Halifax play rugby on a Sunday.

I felt like a single parent at the age of 23 with two boys.

When we went out, which was rarely, I would organise a babysitter. I'd get dressed up, pick up the babysitter, get the bus into Halifax, and meet him in the pub. He'd be there with his friends, and they'd probably been in the pub since 4.30, so when I arrived, they were already drunk. He'd usually have one drink and say, 'Shall we go home?' There was no way, after three hours of preparation for my one night out, that I was going home. I didn't go out every week, in fact, it was more like once a month so he would go home, and I'd stay out. And for those wiser than I was at the time, this was the crack that started the downfall of our relationship.

I asked him if he would stop watching rugby on a Sunday and he said yes, but he was so hungover on the Sunday from his 'playing rugby,' that it was hardly worth the effort.

Daniel used to go to a childminder after school. We both worked in Elland and just after I'd passed my driving test, I used to take the car and drop my husband at work.

On numerous occasions, he'd leave me sitting in the car outside his work whilst he was talking to his boss. For hours!

When I think about it now, I think, 'Why did I tolerate that?' It makes me want to cry. Why didn't I just drive off? I taught him to treat me like this. I taught him to come home on time to eat our meal together, so I know that I could have taught him to leave work on time. I certainly would have done that now.

Why didn't I go to the door and say, 'Come on we've got our boy to collect, we're going to be late.' But I didn't. I sat and waited for him. Stewing. And because I let him get away with it, he carried on doing it.

I would never let anyone treat me like that now. Ever!

Even with all this going on, I still loved him. Yes, we had our ups and downs, as all couples do, and I was desperate for a little girl. So, we decided to try one more time for a girl.

Imagine my delight when we had our gorgeous little girl. She was perfect in every way. As she grew up, she and I were inseparable. She followed me around like a little shadow. I couldn't even go to the loo without her being behind me.

But things in the marriage were getting worse.

We'd got to the stage where it was not working. He was getting promotions at work, and spending more and more time there, and I felt like an unpaid single parent.

I was taking care of three children. Trying to go to college full-time, and I had a part-time job at weekends so that I had some of my own money.

Something snapped. I think I had a breakdown.

I remember standing by the front door, trying to breathe. I couldn't catch my breath. I rang the doctors and was trying to talk to them on the phone, and he told me I was having a panic attack.

Things were just going from bad to worse.

I told him that I'd had enough. I needed some time to think. I booked myself into a small hotel in Bridlington, overnight to collect my thoughts.

After finishing work at 6 pm at Grattan Catalogue, I drove in the dark to Bridlington.

When I arrived, the lady who ran the hotel said to me, 'I've had a call from someone saying he's your husband, he was checking that it was a single reservation. Just thought I should let you know.'

He didn't trust me. He thought I was going with someone else. Just another body blow to the whole relationship. That Sunday morning, I walked for miles on the beach. My head was in a million pieces. I was very aware that I was at a crucial crossroads, and any decisions that I made today, would shape the rest of my and my family's life.

But I wasn't thinking straight. I felt numb.

I arrived back home that evening after the children had gone to bed, and in tears, told him that I'd had enough. I couldn't continue like this. He asked me if I would consider going to counselling, and I said yes, but I already knew that the damage had been done. All those years of being treated like a skivvy had taken its toll, and I couldn't continue in a soul-less marriage.

When we went to see the counsellor, he encouraged us to swap roles. And asked my ex to think about what it would be like if he were me. Standing by the sink washing up and putting his tea on the table. What would he think of me?

That exercise was valuable. He broke down in tears, full of remorse about the way he had treated me. But it was too late. The damage had been done. I couldn't feel anything. I was numb. Like I was on autopilot and no matter what anyone did, it wouldn't have changed my mind.

On New Year's Day, he moved out of the house and went to stay with his mum for a while.

I know he was struggling because he rang me, all the time. We tried every which way to get the arrangements to see the children right, but at every angle, he'd scupper them.

He was turning up at the house drunk, phoning me at all hours of the day and night. He refused to fill in any of the child support agency forms so that he didn't have to pay maintenance. He was a mess.

Marilyn Monroe Moment

" Get your glad rags on, we're going out, "she said. 'We haven't been out in ages.'

It was the end of August and it had been eight months since we'd split up. It was my ex-husband's birthday, and I needed a well-deserved distraction and a bit of downtime. I was working hard. Art college through the day, Grattan call centre from 5 pm till 9 pm, and three children, I was exhausted. Mum said she'd have the children overnight.

I caught the bus into town and met my friend in Portman & Pickles. The pub where I used to work with her when she was my boss.

We usually visited a few of the Tetley pubs. We knew all the staff and landlords of the local hostelries.

It was getting late. She told me that she was meeting a new chap later that evening, he was out with one of his friends, and did I want to come along?

Mum had the children, I'd got a pass, and the alcohol was flowing, so I accepted.

We went to the nightclub and had a few drinks, and she seemed taken by her new chap. Which left me chatting with his friend. At the end of the night, he asked me if I wanted to dance.

And as we were dancing, he said, 'It's my birthday today.' I nearly dropped to the floor! As it was my ex-husband's birthday too, another significant day to get through. Another milestone. All I could think was. Oh no! Another Virgo.

My head was in a bit of a tailspin because I liked him.

At the end of the evening, he asked me if I'd like to go back to his place with him, just for a coffee you understand. I had no intention of sleeping with him, so, I got into a taxi with him.

He made me feel at ease. We talked loads, he poured me another drink and one thing led to another. I was nervous, not having done anything like this for a long time.

Early the following morning as the sun rose, I woke thinking about getting back to reality. The kids were at my mum's. I'd left my car at King Cross and needed to go and collect it. I knew that it was two adults enjoying each other's company, so I said goodbye, not even giving him my number.

I was wearing a short lime green dress. And as I ran across the road to get my car the wind blew and caught my dress and lifted it. It was a bit like a Marilyn Monroe moment. He told me years later, that he sat in his car watching me, and laughed his head off when that happened. He knew then that he was falling in love with me.

I had no intention of getting back in touch with him. It was a bit of fun. I was busy. He worked nights, and it would never work. But a couple of days later, my friend rang me to ask if she could give him my number. I was flattered. He was nice, and we went out together a few times after that.

In total, I'd been a single mum, in the family home, looking after the children for 11 months. Trying to make it work. But something happened on Bonfire Night that would change things forever.

Bonfire Night

I wanted to take the children to a bonfire. It was my birthday weekend, and I usually ended up in a pair of wellies and a hat, and gloves, at a bonfire.

I'd asked the new chap if he wanted to come with us. It was the first time he'd met the children, so it was a big deal. The children had a great time, but it was late, so I needed to get them to bed.

Then there was banging at the front door. It was my ex-husband, he was drunk, saying that he wanted to see the children. I had to let him in because he would wake the little ones up. He asked, if could he go upstairs to say goodnight to our daughter.

At this stage, my new chap had said his goodbyes. We knew it was only going to exacerbate the situation even more.

I told him that he could go up and see our daughter, but if he woke her, he'd be in big trouble. The next thing I knew, he had her in his arms, running down the street with her. It was winter, she didn't have a coat on, and he was drunk!

I had no option but to call the police.

The police found him hiding behind a bush at the end of the street and brought them both back.

We spent about an hour in mediation with them, and he finally calmed down and our daughter was safely tucked back up in bed.

But as soon as the police left, he started again, telling me that he couldn't cope with being a part-time parent.

I'd had enough. I snapped.

From New Year's Eve to Bonfire Night this incessant drunken, verbal battering had worn me down. He'd ring me in the middle of the night, and turn up at the house at all times of the day and night.

I'd lost 2 and a half stones in weight. I couldn't hold my job down; I was struggling with my art course and was miserable.

I asked him if he was serious about not being able to cope with being a part-time parent.

Because we couldn't go on like this. I told him that he couldn't change his mind tomorrow when he was sober. There was no going back from this.

It felt like another defining moment where you know that the decision you make, will change your life forever.

I packed a bag, I gave him the keys to the house, and I drove away.

I needed some space to think. I needed to be out of the way of the constant verbal and emotional battering. When I think about this now, I know that I'd had a breakdown.

I just couldn't take any more. I wasn't making this decision for me alone; I was making it for our children too. Because he involved them in every argument, every altercation. I knew what we were doing was damaging the way that they would turn out. I kept asking him to leave the children out of it, but he knew that the biggest impact on me would be through the children.

I moved in with the new chap. It felt like the right thing to do because he worked nights, it meant that we didn't see that much of each other. He'd be sleeping, whilst I was up and out of the house during the day. He had a dog called Zak. I walked that dog for hours and hours. Just thinking and trying to clear my head. The sadness had taken hold of my body so deeply, that I had difficulty thinking straight at all.

Then one night at about 10 pm, the house phone rang. It was my ex-husband. I couldn't believe that he had got hold of the number. When I asked how he got it, he said that he knew his address, so he'd trawled through the phone book until he found the number. The phone book had thousands and thousands of numbers in it. If he had trawled the phone book, it would have taken him days to do that.

He asked me again if I'd come back. If I'd change my mind and return home.

I told him that I'd made my mind up and I couldn't do that.

There were a couple of other instances during that period from November to January that I remember vividly.

My daughter was at the college nursery. She got a place there when I was doing my art course. I would drop her off in the building across the road and go into my classes.

But at this stage, I wasn't going to college. At first, I would go in for a couple of hours, but my mind wasn't in the right place to do the course, so I'd go home.

Mum and Dad were both working full time and between them, they came up with a plan to try and get me to see the children. Mum asked me if I would pick my daughter up from their house that morning and take her to the nursery, so I did.

I was like a robot. I put her in her car seat. I drove to the college nursery. Took her in, didn't say a word, and then left.

I had depression. I knew I had because there was simply no emotion. I'd blocked it all out. When I reflect on this, it was exactly the way I was when I'd had Daniel.

No emotion. Nothing to say to anyone. No feeling.

I was so thin. I was poorly. I'd lost so much weight with all the stress of it.

A few weeks later, Mum and Dad asked me to come to their house to try and find a solution with my ex. I arrived and sat down. My dad and my ex were talking about different scenarios. It felt like there were talking about me, whilst I wasn't there.

I could feel myself rocking back and forwards in the chair. Like you do with a child to comfort them. They were trying to fix something that was way too broken to fix that easily.

Here's a poem that I wrote around this time.

From New Year's Eve to Bonfire Night

From New Year's Eve to Bonfire Night

You stole the sunlight from my life.

The stress, anger, hurt, and pain, added to the turmoil of the daily drain.

You stole my life, so I had to flee.

Thousands of miles just to be free

Of your bitter and twisted sense of betrayal

Dragging everyone in, truly destroying that veil.

Now everyone thinks you're the lord of the manor.

Talking at people, waving your banner

But by winning the fight, they lost the war.

On that Bonfire Night in 1994.

Your drunken revenge, you meant to sow.

Crippling your family, but how were you to know?

Your male ego is in shreds

So, who can blame

any natural husband whose wife puts him to shame?

18 months on, I'm picking up the remnants of my life.

Since that fateful day when I was no longer your wife

Home is now Africa, the land of the free?

This is where I'm happiest, just being me.

Cape Town

My new chap and I had been seeing each other for a little while.

It was January 1995 and throughout the whole break up with my ex-husband he had been right by my side, listening to every single event and challenge that I'd been through. In my mind, I was trying to get through the most horrific separation and divorce that I'd ever heard of.

My ex-husband had tried every trick in the book to break me.

Not paying maintenance.

Phoning me at all times of day and night.

Turning up at the house drunk, on many occasions.

But mostly, using the children against me, which of course he knew, would hurt me more than anything in the world.

This new guy was my shoulder throughout this painful journey. He was my rock. A beautiful soul.

I knew that he adored me, and I thought he was the one.

That Christmas was the toughest Christmas I'd ever had. The first one without my babies.

To help, he'd arranged for us to go to Scotland to a cottage in the middle of nowhere.

We took his dog and even our own Christmas tree.

It was very romantic, but I remember putting the tree up and thinking, 'This is like torture, I should be doing this with my children.' I was heartbroken. In pieces. My world was shattered, and I was struggling to make sense of any of it.

During our stay in Scotland, I told him that I had decided, in January that I was going to South Africa. Back to where I'd grown up, to get away from "all this shit," so that I could heal.

I'd spent the last couple of weeks, trying to track down some friends that I used to go to school with. This was in the days before the internet, so I had to use my detective skills.

I rang international directory enquiries. I gave them the names of three girls that I was close to at school. With two of them, there was no luck at all, but with the remaining one, I was able to get her mum's telephone number. I picked up the phone and dialled the number. Her mum answered and told me that her daughter had moved to Cape Town. She said she would call her and ask whether it was ok to give me her number. Could I call back in a couple of days, and all being well, she would pass her number on to me?

I called back a couple of days later as agreed, and she said that her daughter was delighted that I'd got back in touch and gave me her number. I called her straight away.

I spent quite a while on the phone explaining what had happened. She was supportive and wonderful. She told me that she was excited to see me again, that I could stay with her for as long as I liked, and that I should keep her informed of the dates and arrangements.

My new chap was devastated when I told him. He told me that he'd always wanted to live abroad, and he wanted to come with me. It would take him some time to get things sorted, so if it was ok, could he follow me on later?

I, of course, said yes.

I sold and/or gave away all my possessions, packed one big suitcase, and on the 6th of January 1995, I boarded a plane to Cape Town.

In my head, I knew that I had to get away from all this pain. It was the year that The World Cup Rugby was being played in South Africa and in my messed-up head I knew that I had to get as far away from my ex-husband as I could before he ruined me forever. I even thought that he may follow me if he knew where I was. Perhaps blending a trip to watch the rugby, with coming to find me. I didn't let anyone know where I was going. As I left the country on that cold January morning, I dropped three letters into a post box.

One to my solicitor, so that he could contact me about my divorce, one to Mum and Dad, and one to my sister. Telling them not to worry, that I was fine, and that I would be in touch when I was settled. That I was going somewhere out of the way, where no one could find me.

There is a bridge in Halifax, called North Bridge, that has a reputation for people jumping off it when they are struggling to cope. Mum told me a couple of years later that she and Dad had seen a girl attempting to jump off the bridge and Mum thought it was me.

I was truly not thinking straight, all I could think was. I must get away!

I remember like it was yesterday, with my Sony Walkman, as I landed at Cape Town airport. As the plane landed, I was listening to Louis Armstrong's Wonderful World with tears streaming down my face.

I spent the first three months healing. I have a photograph of my first few days in Cape Town with my friend from school and I look about 20 years older than I was. They say, don't they, that a picture tells a thousand words? Well, I can see the pain in my body in that photograph.

When I first arrived, we stayed in a tiny one-bedroom cottage. But she had plans for us to move into a larger house with an extra bedroom and a garden for her dog.

Soon after I'd arrived, I called down to the P.O. Box to see if I had any post. I'd received a letter from my dad. He'd been into the solicitors and got the address from him.

My dad never wrote letters. He is dyslexic, so for him to write a letter was very significant. He told me that he loved me, that he missed me and to take care of myself.

My dad didn't do emotions. To see his words, written on that page, was very emotional. I stood in the street with tears rolling down my face. The last time he'd told me that he loved me was when I'd tried to commit suicide at the age of 17. Living there was tough. I was thousands of miles away from my family and friends. My friend had been so kind by moving house and helping me. I couldn't thank her enough.

During my time there I met another girl called Lee. I got on with her well. We'd go second-hand furniture hunting in her bright yellow Datsun car.

She loved music and we spent lots of time together over the next few months.

She taught me how to play guitar. I have fond memories of our time together.

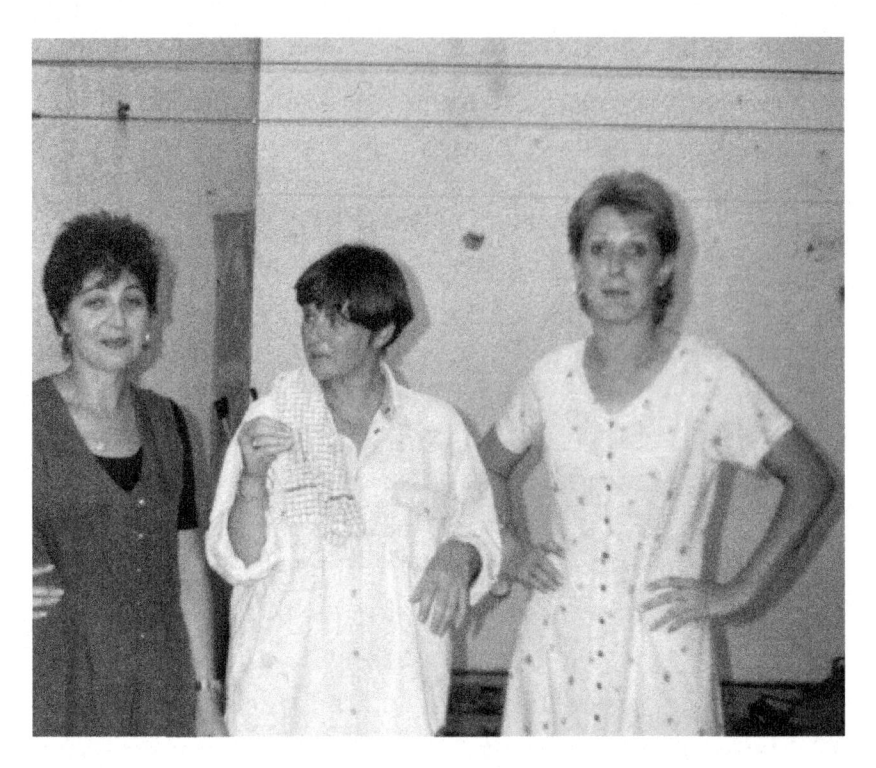

I'm the one on the right with my hands on my hips. We were in the process of moving to a bigger house with an extra bedroom.

After about three months I moved into my own place, a little one-bedroomed apartment above a chemist in Sea Point. My next-door neighbours were a gay couple. One worked as a waiter in the Spur Restaurant and the other was a merchandiser for Woolworths (the Marks and Spencer equivalent in South Africa.)

They both looked out for me. I didn't have a washing machine, so I'd take my laundry around and Albie would encourage me to taste his baking or ply me with wine, whilst the next load of washing finished.

Over time I was starting to build a new life for myself and heal my wounds. My children were never far from my mind. I remember one day on the beach, there was a beautiful little girl who looked just like my daughter, and I burst into tears.

It's true what they say. You can't run away from your problems. You can try to change your life as much as possible, but you will always take you with you. The saying. You can run but 'you can't hide' is very true, and sooner or later you must face up to your demons.

I didn't have the energy to face up to them whilst going through what I was going through at the time. I needed healing time.

The mind is a fascinating thing, isn't it? It has weird and wonderful ways of helping you cope. I'd almost sort of blocked out my life in the UK.

In hind-site, I realise that it was helping me heal.

For those of you that judge me for leaving my children. My response is, walk a mile in my shoes before judging me for doing what I did.

I believe that everything happens for a reason. I have learned to not judge anyone for the actions that they take in their life.

Everyone makes all kinds of decisions based on where they are at that time in their life. Perhaps because of the influences and experiences that they have had in their lives when they were children. (Wounded child stories.) Because of my experiences, I will never judge anyone for the actions that they take. No matter what they are. You are simply doing the best you can, with what you have.

I felt free. Alive. For the very first time in a long time, I knew that my children were far better off with a mum that was alive and on the other side of the world than one that was no longer with us. My decision was one of survival.

Whilst living in my flat, a few months after arriving, I received a call from my sister. We were inseparable when we were younger. My only sibling, so we shared everything. She had a daughter who was 3 months younger than my daughter, so we were very close. She was the only one who had my number. I trusted her with my life, but that phone call changed everything about our relationship.

Years ago, when you received an overseas call, there was a tiny delay as the call connected. I knew it was her before she began to speak. She was sobbing on the phone. I thought something had happened to one of the children because she was so upset. But she said, "I've got something to tell you. I'm seeing John." It was so far removed from what I could get my head around, I said, "John who?"

She said, my ex-husband's name. I started laughing. I couldn't believe what she was telling me.

I remember saying that it was ok, but when I'd put the phone down, and thought it through, I realised the implications of what she had told me. What an impact it would have on my life.

I rang her back and said, "You do realise that man will never be welcome in my life, don't you?" And you have seen everything that I have gone through over the last 12 months? She said, 'Yes, but he's kind and I miss your children.'

I was numb. I couldn't believe what she was telling me. I felt betrayed. She was the only person that I trusted. I thought I could trust her with my life.

I told her my deepest secrets. She knew me like no other. That one decision would change not just our lives, but the whole of our family's lives forever.

A few months later, I went down to the PO box that I'd rented to receive letters from my solicitor regarding the divorce and from my sister.

There was a letter from her. Tucked away in the back corner of the PO Box.

Inside her letter was a letter from my ex-husband.

It felt like a Trojan horse.

She had done what I asked, by not giving anyone my address, but the very next worst thing in the world was to enclose a letter from him!

She'd told him that she had my address. That she knew where I was.

In my head, I thought if she's told him that, what else has she told him?

What other 'afterglow' stories has she shared with him?

I could not understand why she would do that.

Where was her loyalty to me?

The only other thing I could think was that she had been influenced by him. He could be very influential when he wanted something. He would stop at nothing to get what he wanted. Perhaps she had no say in it at all?

But I could not believe that of her. She could be very strong-willed. The complete opposite to me. Deep, dark, and secretive. She had always kept all her cards to her chest. One thing was for sure, I would never be able to trust her again, as long as I lived.

Here's the thing though, it wasn't until having done my energy medicine work that I realise that because she had a very similar upbringing to me, her distorted energy had manifested differently. She was simply doing the best she could with the life skills she had learnt.

I had no idea, of the long-term implications of their decision, and how it would impact our lives, for the rest of our lives.

After my chap had got all his affairs in order, he came over to join me in May of that year. And shortly afterward we found a beautiful house at the bottom of Table Mountain in a place called Oranjezicht.

The couple who owned the house had an idyllic lifestyle and spent half of the year in Cape Town and the other half in Spain. They needed someone to house-sit whilst they were away. It was perfect for us, with a pool and two bedrooms.

Because he was a qualified engineer, he found work quickly and started working for a company in Simon's Town, just outside Cape Town, making guns for the South African armed forces.

I found a job working for an ex-pat. She was an accommodation consultant. Cape Town is the equivalent of Brighton in the UK. There is a large gay community, and everyone came to Cape Town for their holidays from December to February. It is a beautiful place.

I worked without a visa, and used a pseudonym so that I didn't get caught by the authorities. I worked hard, helping people find monthly, weekly, and daily accommodation lets, in hotels and private houses. It was a challenging job because it wasn't 9- 5 and my boss said that if I had the work ethic of a Brit, then I could make serious money. She wasn't wrong.

I loved that job. We got to see some amazing sites in Cape Town. We made the most of having to check out the hotels to see if they were up to scratch for our demanding clients. We sampled lots of wonderful drinks and meals in hostelries all over the Cape.

At that time there were lots of film crews organising photography shoots. They were willing to pay thousands of South African Rands for daily rentals of picture-perfect lodges and homes with the perfect setting.

Our favourite thing to do on a Friday after work was Sundowners.

I have fond memories of getting on the back of his motorbike and driving to Camps Bay on a Friday evening after work to watch the sun go down and enjoy a few beers. Things were looking good, but as with most things, everything would come to an end.

Later that year I reconnected with my mum. She and Dad had also split up that year. She said she missed me and wanted to come and see me, and was it ok to come across and spend a month with us.

It was lovely to see her, and we had the space for her to stay. We were her personal tour guides, and together with my neighbours, who loved my mum, we showed her the time of her life.

It was during her stay that she showed me lots of photos of the children. I could see how they were growing up without me. I missed them dreadfully. My visa was running out, and by the end of her stay, we'd agreed that I would return.

It broke my heart to leave my love on his own in Cape Town, but I needed to deal with my demons and face up to reality. I was strong enough now, to be able to handle the situation and decided to return. I'd been in Cape Town for a total of 16 months.

When I returned to the UK, I had £5 in my pocket. I stayed at mum's and needed to find work quickly. I took anything to keep the wolf from the door. I phoned my sister first. I'm guessing that because she didn't hear that distinctive long-distance pause on the phone as she picked up the phone, the first thing she said was, 'Where are you?' I said, "I'm back in the UK", and you could cut the air with a knife. What I had not realised at that point was that she was about to move in with my ex-husband. The next task was to buck up the courage to contact my ex-husband to ask if I could see the children.

I arranged to meet him in a pub, near where he was now living. Ironically it was a house that we had looked at whilst we were still together, although, what I now know about my ex-husband is that nothing was ever by accident.

We talked uncomfortably for a little while, and he asked me if I would like to see where they were living. I said yes because I wanted to see where my children lived and what their home looked like.

I was driving Mum's car, so I followed him to the house.

I will never forget this moment as long as I live.

He stood with his arm resting on the old fireplace and said, "I've asked her to marry me you know, and she's said yes."

I was speechless. But tried not to show any emotion. I replied, "Well if you think I could ever condone that relationship, then you are sadly mistaken."

As I drove away from the house, I knew that my life and access to my children would be a challenge until they were old enough to make their own decisions.

I was devastated and broke, angry, and frustrated by the whole situation, but at least I was healed and able to deal with it from a stronger perspective.

I felt he played on my weaknesses. He told me that I needed to pay maintenance for the children, and although it wasn't a lot of money to him, it was an amount equal to a week's pay for me.

He also told me that if we went to court, it would cost me a lot more than I was paying and he wanted me to pay it cash, in his hand every month.

I was livid!

Even after everything we'd been through, he was still trying to control me.

In hindsight, I should have taken it to court, at least that way it would have been binding and I wouldn't have had to go through all the emotional trauma of paying him in his hand every month. I felt like he was controlling me still, even after all this time.

I vowed, from that moment on, that no man would ever have control over my finances. I have a saying, which is, "I can tie my own shoelaces."

Financial independence is one of my key traits because of these experiences.

It was a lesson I had to learn.

The other ingredient in the whole messy mix was that you may remember me saying that my sister had a daughter, who was only 3 months younger than my daughter.

He told me that if I wanted to see my children, then I had to have my niece at the same time. Imagine how that would make you feel. I didn't decide to move in with my brother-in-law and raise my sister's children. So why should I have to look after her daughter? Don't get me wrong I loved that girl, like she was my own, and had I been given the choice I would have had her too, but to have the choice taken away from you and be forced to take her, was yet another control issue.

My niece is a very social creature and loved to show her emotions so when she was little, she was happy to come for a cuddle and sit on my knee. My daughter was different, in that she was a much more closed book and always had been. I remember sitting my niece on my lap and my daughter watching, and inside yearning for it to be my baby girl who was sitting right here. I knew that if my niece was coming with us, I would be constantly trying to juggle the connection between them both, and I needed to make focusing on connecting with my children my priority. It was an emotional roller coaster.

Because I resented having no choice in taking my niece, it damaged my niece and my relationship too. It's taken a very long time for us to have a good relationship because of the decisions of others.

That Easter we had arranged for me to have the children for the whole of the Easter weekend. I was beside myself with excitement.

I borrowed Mum's car, drove up to the house, and knocked on the door. There was no answer. I waited for about half an hour and they didn't return.

I went back home to Mum. It was in the days before mobiles, so I rang the house phone and left a message. Still no reply. For the whole of that afternoon, I kept ringing every half an hour. What they didn't know was that every time I left a message, the phone took a little bit longer to record my message, so I knew when they'd listened to all my messages.

As soon as I knew they were home, I got in the car and drove like a mad woman up to the house and banged on the door. All the lights were on. Everyone was home and I could hear my sister shout, 'It's our Fran!'

My ex answered the door and as soon as he opened it, I wedged my foot in the door so that he couldn't close it.

I refused to leave until I had collected my children.

We had reached a stalemate. He said that he would call the police and I said, 'Call them!'

After some considerable time, we had been talking to a police officer on the phone who had listened to both sides of the story. He encouraged my ex to agree for me to return first thing the following morning to collect my children.

I had knocked on the door so hard that day, that I had taken all the skin off my knuckles. I looked like I'd been fighting. Which I had. Fighting to see my children.

Imagine having to ask for permission to see your children from your sister?

What I didn't realise until years later was that it was her that was making the rules behind the scenes, not him.

Logically, that made complete sense to me, because my ex was a workaholic and he needed someone to take care of the children because he had always worked such long hours.

I once bumped into him in Halifax town centre on a night out, and I asked him, 'Of all the women in the world, why did he choose my sister?

He said, 'Because of the children.'

Words of Wisdom

I can honestly say that this was one of the most emotionally challenging periods of my life. I wasn't coping very well, and to dull the pain, I was going out and getting drunk. Around this time, I met a guy who was a regular in the pub where I worked. He was funny and made me laugh. He'd buy me a drink if it was his round, and goofed around with a group of his friends. At last orders, he would always buy two pints, as if one wasn't enough to drink in the 20 minutes that it took until kicking out time at 11 pm. It felt like he was the tonic that I needed to forget everything. Within a couple of weeks of our meeting, he asked me to marry him. He almost asked it as a throwaway comment when we'd both been drinking one night. I hadn't even lived with him, and I said yes. He had a lovely little house on the opposite side of town, and after we got married, I was going to move in with him.

Because I was still living at Mum's, I used to spend quite a bit of time at his house. He had a big dining kitchen, and I love entertaining, so I used to make food and invite a group of friends over. One of the guys was a fabulous musician and I loved that group of friends. I felt like I'd found somewhere I belonged.

He had a good job. He was a joiner and a great group of friends. We decided that we would get married in Scarborough and go for the weekend.

I remember about a month before the wedding, my mum warned me against him. She said, 'He doesn't have a good reputation.' A friend of hers knew him and he was a drunk and a lad around town, and she thought I was making a big mistake. I, of course, did not listen to her and went ahead with the wedding.

We asked close friends to join us. And booked Scarborough Registry Office. We travelled from Halifax on the morning of the wedding, and because one of the guests was very late in arriving at our house, we were running late to get there.

The girls in one car and the boys in another. We were giddy with excitement, but we were very late and nearly lost our wedding slot. My new groom's nephew was always playing silly tricks and was full of fun and high jinks. As we said our vows and the groom pulled our rings from the ring box, his nephew had placed a cheap price tag on his ring as he took it out of the box. I also recollect how the two rings were the complete opposite ends of the scale in size. Mine – the tiniest ring size and his – the largest. We stayed in a little hotel in town. I'd booked a lovely restaurant for our meal, and this is where I'd prepared a poem that I wrote out in calligraphy to give to him on the day of our wedding.

We went to the fairground. We called at Robin Hoods Bay for a couple of drinks and had a great time in Scarborough that night.

The following morning, we decided to come down to breakfast in our pyjamas. This is when we cut our wedding cake.

It was the weekend of my birthday, and we were due to have a big party back in Halifax the weekend after, for a larger gathering of family and friends.

He made me laugh. He took my mind off everything that was going on with my children. I was getting drunk with him on Thursday, Friday, Saturday, and Sunday nights, and somehow managing to get into work on a Monday morning. I was slowly on a downward spiral. The alcohol was numbing the pain. I was starting to see the children again but was struggling with being the absent parent.

I got to see them once a week, and the pain of reconnecting with them was so tough. I'd blocked off my emotions. They were crying out to be loved by me. For me to fight for them, and I couldn't do it. I didn't have the strength to fight both my ex-husband and my sister. I felt like they had joined forces. He'd taken my one true ally away (my sister) and I didn't have anyone I could talk to who understood me. I felt like she was a spy and joined the other side. I felt betrayed and unloved by the one person that I thought I could rely on.

I moved into his house as soon as we got back from Scarborough. And for the next couple of months, things were fine(ish). He would sleep in at weekends until lunchtime, just in time to get up and come around, in preparation for the next drinking session.

I was sorting out some paperwork that had been piling up on the side in the kitchen and found some old bank statements and I could see that he was way behind with his mortgage payments.

Sex was non-existent, because of the drinking. He told me after we'd got married that it was hard work for him because he had to do all the work!

Then we had a two-week break for Christmas. We were drinking heavily. Going out nearly every night.

I went downstairs to the cellar one day to put something away. There, lined up, in rows were lots of electric drills, saws, and work tools.

I estimate about 25 different types of Dewalt products. I knew from working with my dad that these things weren't cheap, and when I came up to the kitchen, I asked him about them. He said, 'Well if the guys on site are silly enough to leave them lying around, then they're going to lose them, aren't they?'

I was flabbergasted and looked at him in horror. I said, 'But these tools are those guys' livelihood!'

I knew from working with my dad that just one of those pieces of kit could cost £500 and that was nearly 25 years ago. To give you some context, the guys that worked for my dad then were earning about £300 per week.

I was so disappointed in him. I lost my respect for him. Those two events made me see the type of man he was. I realised I did not know him at all. I was so disappointed in him. How you do anything is how you do everything. Because of the drama that I'd had in my life so far, I realised that what came out of his mouth was a pack of lies. He was lazy and a drunk and my mum was 100% right. But I suppose when I'd blocked out my emotions to protect myself, I'd also blocked out my intuitive self. The one who knows the truth. The one who can make informed decisions that were best for me in the long term. The cracks were already starting to show.

The final straw came at the end of that Christmas holiday.

We'd been into town with some friends. He was friendly with a girl across the road and had knocked on the door to ask if she'd like to come across for some drinks, but she didn't answer the door. I asked him to stop banging because he'd wake up all the neighbours, and perhaps she didn't want to come across. 'Just leave it.' I said. But he insisted on making a spectacle of himself.

It was at that moment when I'd had enough. Like a great big lightning bolt from the sky. What was I doing?

I saw the rest of my life panning out in front of me with a man who did not deserve me. I would constantly be mopping up disasters and my reputation would be in pieces living with this man.

I felt dreadful after two weeks of drinking. And immediately saw the similarities to my first-ever boyfriend. It wouldn't be long before I would be the downtrodden housewife, living from one week to another in a mountain of debt because he was drinking away all his wages.

I rang his nephew and asked if he wouldn't mind taking me to my friend's house. I explained everything that had happened. The nephew was very considered in his answer and said, 'Frances, he's my uncle, and if I take you from him, he will never forgive me. Please ask someone else or phone a taxi.'

I phoned a taxi and called my friend, a girl who had been to the wedding. The last thing I saw as I drove away in that taxi, was him standing at the door, stark naked, shouting, 'Don't go! Please come back.'

I stayed at my friend's house for a while, until I got myself sorted out.

A couple of weeks later I decided to get a divorce. I knew that I did not want to go back to him. Marrying him in the first place was another big mistake. I went to see a solicitor and he advised, that because we'd only been married for 8 weeks, we could apply for an annulment. We would say that the wedding had not been consummated. The irony of that made me smile because it wasn't that far from the truth.

I spoke to him about it, telling him that I would pay for the divorce, and he said, 'Daddy's little rich girl. You always get what you want. If it doesn't go in the local papers and you pay for it, I'm fine about it.'

I got back to the solicitor, and we decided to go to the Leeds Court House because that way, it wouldn't be reported in the local newspaper.

I met my solicitor in Leeds a few months later and stood before the judge to explain what had happened. I don't know if he didn't believe me, but my case was thrown out of that court and my solicitor said that we'd need to go to another courthouse further down the road and repeat the process.

The entire experience was crazy, from beginning to end. It started just as quickly as it finished, and until now, I've put it right to the back of my mind. Never wanting to think about how stupid I was, ever again.

What I have learnt is that if my mum was giving me some advice, then I'd better listen in the future. She was very wise.

Reconnecting with Cape Town Man

I was living on my own and missed him. He had, after all, been there for me through thick and thin. I'd been the one to call it off after a few months when I got home. It was difficult to keep up a long-distance relationship, because then, overseas calls cost a fortune, and letters were taking at least a week to arrive.

I was trying to protect my heart. I couldn't stand not being with him, and I knew that I was going to stay in the UK forever. I'd started to connect with my children and would never leave them again.

I'd found a new place to live, and I was curious about how he was doing, so I reached out to him. What happened next, felt like it was meant to be, because I bumped into his friend (the one who had dated my friend, when we first met.) I asked how he was and said that I'd like to contact him. So, he must have mentioned it to him, the next time he was in touch, because, out of the blue I received an email. It had been such a long time since I'd spoken to his friend, that I'd decided that he must not want to get in touch. I'd almost given up hope of hearing from him.

He said, how it had been such a lovely surprise to hear from me, he asked how I'd been and what I was up to. I'd been very ill. I'd lost a ton of weight and was struggling to keep down my job because I was having heavy periods and debilitating panic attacks.

My body was going into melt down because of the stress of losing my children. Add to the mix, the battle I was having with my ex and sister, and you can imagine how I was. I was drinking too much to dull the reality of my life and generally, just keeping my head above water.

He told me that he was back in the UK! The guy that he worked for in South Africa was an ex-pat, and because of legislation, he had decided to move his company to the UK. His boss loved living by the sea, so they relocated to Bexhill-on-Sea. He was back in this country, and I never even knew!

We kept in touch through emails and phone calls. After a couple of months, he told me that he was coming home to see his parents, and would he be able to come up and see me.

My heart leaped with joy! Perhaps, there might be a slim chance that we could start to rekindle the beautiful relationship that we'd once had.

This guy had been my warrior. My saviour. And I thought that maybe he could be again. I missed him so much.

That first meeting was special. He drove up to see me, and I remember vividly, as he walked through the door to my flat. The connection. It was electric. His eyes were deep pools of brown, and as I looked into them, it was like I'd come home. The smell of his body, as he held me, and kissed me so passionately was something that I yearned for. My soul connected to him in a way that I cannot describe. He knew me.

Over the next few months, we spent as much time as we could together. We took it in turns to drive between Halifax and Bexhill-on-Sea.

One weekend it was his turn to come to me. I was working at the Halifax Bank in the marketing team, and he was coming up by train. He was meeting me from work. I couldn't sit still. I kept looking out of the window to see if he'd arrived. My heart was pounding like an excited puppy. They were magical times.

During one of our conversations, I told him about my Milk Tray Man fantasy. Where I imagined a man in a black polo-neck jumper jumping through the window of my bedroom with a box of chocolates.

One day at work there was a parcel for me. I got a call to ask if I'd go down to the mail room to collect it.

To my surprise, when I opened the parcel, it was two boxes of Milk Tray chocolates. The message on the top was one box for you and one for the team. Because I'd told him that mail room security was strict, he pushed a secret card in the box for me, with a hand-drawn picture of a Milk Tray man, and written 'All because the lady loves xxxx.'

Another beautiful love gesture that he made, was to meet him in Paris.

He'd arranged and sent me my tickets, and I was to meet him at Gare du Nord train station.

I was so excited. He treated me like a Princess. He loved Paris, so he knew it like the back of his hand and took me to some amazing places. We went to Mont Martre, at the top of the hill in the middle of Paris where all the artists congregate. He also took me to the cemetery, which sounds a bit strange, but there are some famous people buried there. Like Edith Piaf, Oscar Wilde, and Jim Morrison. What he didn't expect whilst we were there, was to see an actual funeral taking place. The coffin was laden with pink roses, and it had only been a few months before, that we had buried my grandma, and her coffin had, had the same roses on the top. I burst into tears. One of the many memories I have of that trip was sitting outside a café, sharing a bottle of wine, when hundreds of roller skaters came hurtling through the city centre.

It's the Parisian thing to do on a Friday evening. Who knew that?

We went back to our hotel room, tired but also looking forward to connecting at a much deeper level.

As we got into bed, and cuddled up, the biggest thunderstorm broke, and whilst we made love, the claps of thunder and bolts of lightning joined forces with us. It felt like the heavens were rejoicing, as our bodies connected at every level.

Parting with him on the Gare Du Nord platform on Sunday was like leaving him in Cape Town. I felt bereft as I sat on that train, with tears streaming down my face.

We started to make plans. He was going to give up his job and move up to Halifax, and we were going to buy a house together.

I'd had some time off work because I was feeling so ill and stayed with him at his stunning ground-floor apartment which looked out onto the sea. He had amazing taste, and his home was like something out of a beautiful home magazine, with candles everywhere and a breathtaking four-poster bed.

One night, I got out of the bath and opened the door to the airing cupboard to get a fresh towel. There were two bunches of red roses, dried up so that the colour was now almost black.

Later that evening as we shared a bottle of wine, I asked him about the roses.

He told me that he'd been having an affair with a married woman. Those roses were bought when she told him she was coming over to see him, but then she'd let him down at the last minute.

I found it so sad that such a beautiful man had put himself in that situation.

The weekend before he was due to move up to Halifax, he asked me if I'd come down to Bexhill and attend his leaving party from work.

We went for a meal, at a nice local restaurant, and I remember sitting opposite this woman that he'd been having the affair with because she worked at the company as him and thinking, I wonder how much he's told her about me?

On the day of the move, I was so excited! Finally, my wish was coming true. The man that I was meant to be with was giving up everything to be with me.

We spent the next 6 months, finding him work, and saving like crazy for the deposit for our house. We moved into our beautiful new home and started to knock down walls and make it our own. The thing that I loved about that house was that it almost expanded with us.

When the children came to stay at weekends, the girls slept in the attic, the boys in the second bedroom, and downstairs in the cellar was a big music room where he stored his guitars and computer.

The following summer I'd arranged to go on a girl's week to Benidorm, it was one of my close friend's birthdays and it was all arranged. We were going for a week of sun, fun, and frivolity. He was not happy.

When I returned, there was a huge bouquet on the kitchen table. I remember him pulling me towards him. Sitting me on his knee and saying, 'I never want to be apart from you again. I've hated every minute of you being away.'

It was such a happy home. We were creating a wonderful life together.

We'd been in the house for about 18 months. It was Christmas Day, and we were sitting in our dressing gowns, cosying up in the lounge in front of the fire, opening our presents, and having our first cuppa of the day, when he got down on one knee and asked me to marry him.

It was a total shock. I cried my eyes out, I was so happy. Of course, I said yes. He produced a beautiful engagement ring which I wore with pride. We talked about getting married on a wine farm out in Stellenbosch near Cape Town.

But things started to get a bit weird. I knew that he stretched the limits when it came to sex. It was never boring. But what I didn't know, was that he was very attracted to porn. It was his dark side. I called him Inspector Gadget because I always knew that he had things that he kept from me, hidden in his 'overcoat.' He had a secretive side to him, and as I got to know him better, I learned more and more about this side of his personality.

He was adventurous in the bedroom and used to push the boundaries. He was fascinated by all things porn related. And slowly, over time, the fascination started to creep further and further into the intimacy of our relationship.

Let's say that I had to say no to quite a few of his requests.

There were a couple of instances where I'd come home from work unexpectedly, and he'd be sitting downstairs with the computer on, watching porn.

I'm not a prude. I get it. But what I didn't like was that the lines were blurring. He asked me if I wanted to share with another couple. When I looked at his conversations online, he was asking them if they'd like to come to our home!

It was starting to get to me. Our intimacy became a marathon. It took hours and hours of seduction. And all the while he was introducing more and more of his 'digital' world into our bed. He asked me if I'd considered having a boob job for example and I just didn't feel like I was enough. And slowly over time, things started to deteriorate. Until I could take no more.

I asked him to move out. I had to sell my beautiful car, to help get the money together to pay him out.

Months later, after I'd got the finances sorted out, we met, in a pub in Sowerby Bridge, where he insisted that I pay him cash.

He turned up in a freshly laundered, white linen shirt and jeans. He knew that was my favourite look for him.

He was a beautiful man, and in hindsight, I wished we'd gone to get help with his addiction. But in those days, it wasn't even a thing that you talked about.

I gave him the envelope, and said, 'I hope you and your broadband are happy together.' He told me that he was moving to Canada. And ironically, it would have destroyed him to share me with someone else.

I was on my own once again, I'd lost the love of my life.

And I haven't seen him since.

The wedding

Ten years after my ex and my sister got together, they decided to get married.

This was a complete shock to me. Based on what I knew about him, I thought he had decided against it.

It was to be in Sienna in Italy. The girls were going to be bridesmaids.

A few weeks before the wedding I received a call from my sister, in tears, asking if I would come to the wedding. You can imagine my response. It was a resounding no! Can you imagine watching my sister getting married to my ex-husband? With my ex-mother-in-law in the audience. No thank you.

I always wondered what would happen when the children were old enough to make their own decisions and look after themselves.

Would their relationship last? Well sure enough as the children got to their late teens, the relationship ended. You can make your own decisions about why.

It's 20 years later now.

There has been a lot of water under the bridge.

Recently, I asked my sister if she could go back to where we were before all of this happened. She said, 'It'll never be the same Fran' and she was right. You see the trust has gone. I felt betrayed by her.

She has had problems with her thyroid. Your thyroids are glands, and your glands communicate directly with your soul.

When your thyroids aren't working properly, it represents unexpressed emotions, either over-functioning or under-functioning, meaning that communication is closed at some level.

Your thyroid is connected to your desire to live and to be involved in your life.

Recently I asked her if we could talk through what had happened in the past and put it to bed once and for all. She said that she didn't want to dwell on the past, and only wanted to look to the future. I was angry with her for her response. I can't make her see that opening and releasing what lies beneath, will help her heal and grow. She must want to do this for herself.

I often wonder who was the most to blame for that episode of my life.

Was it my ex, my sister, or me?

My sister is blood. She should have never made that decision.

But my ex was devious, and calculating, he knew exactly what he was doing when he made that decision.

Every family gathering, was torture when they turned up together, I felt like I was walking into the lion's den. It felt like they were ganging up on me. It was always them against me.

CHAPTER EIGHT

Let the healing begin

Apple crumble moments

I was working at the Halifax Bank and at around the age of 40, started having problems with my periods. Bleeding for 3 weeks out of 4, every month. And as you can imagine, I felt permanently exhausted. Someone at work suggested that I visit a homeopath. I made an appointment because I was desperate to get it sorted out.

The homeopath was amazing. After sharing some of my stories, she said, 'I'm not a counsellor, but your womb is crying out to be healed, because of the loss of your children.'

She suggested that I go and see a counsellor. She recommended a wonderful woman called Jane, who I saw every Tuesday evening after work. One of the sessions will stay with me for the rest of my life.

I was sharing how I was struggling to connect with my daughter. And how one evening, after school, I'd made the evening meal as usual. The boys were upstairs on the Play Station, and my daughter was sitting at the table waiting for the apple crumble to come out of the oven. She started to open up, talking about everyday things that had happened at school.

Jane said, 'You need to create more apple crumble moments.'

She thought that because my daughter was so young when we had split up, she had absorbed the trauma. She was 2 and a half, and at that time, just learning to communicate. When there was such negative communication in the only world that she knew, she was struggling to articulate what she needed, and the negative trauma was stuck.

When my ex and other adults were speaking badly of me, or even if they weren't, she absorbed the energy of the situation, and I was seen as a bad person. She couldn't be seen talking to me, so she would only open up to me when there was no one else around.

Oh, my goodness. What a revelation! I was over the moon to have had such a breakthrough.

You can bet your bottom dollar that I did my absolute best to create more and more of those apple crumble moments with my daughter.

My opinion about talking therapy is that it helped to get things off my chest, but the breakthrough came for me when I discovered energy medicine.

To be a good energy healer, you need to have healed your wounds.

Energy healing finds emotions that are trapped deep within your energy system and gently, helps to release them and give them back to the person that gave them to you, with love.

This means that if it's something that has been passed from one generation to another, you heal your DNA lineage too.

Energy healing doesn't give you what you want, it gives you what you need. I have many case studies of women who have come to me for one thing and feel so much better because something else has healed inside their bodies. To give you an example of this, read Natalie's story at the end of the book.

I did try other methods of counselling, but I seemed to go round and round in circles, having to share the same information with different people. It was confusing at some points, because of the conflicting advice and questioning.

Online Dating

I started online dating when I lived in Morley just outside Leeds. I was working as a marketing manager for Leeds College of Art. Work was good because work didn't need my emotions, I rolled my sleeves up and got on with it.

But when it came to my love life, it was a completely different story.

All those dates, with all those fascinating characters. People found my dating stories interesting, and I would always get asked about my latest experiences by friends and family. But it got to the stage where I felt like my love life was for their entertainment.

I wanted someone wonderful to settle down with, but every time, there seemed to be some reason that it did not quite work out.

I wasn't fussy, I just wanted someone normal, lovely, and kind.

Surely it could not be that hard to find the one.

I tried paid-for sites, and free sites, swiping left, and swiping right, and always talked to them on the phone first to get a feel for their energy before I made the effort to go and meet them face to face.

On one of these dates, one guy's photograph was so out of date, that I walked straight past him at the train station because he had put some much weight on since his photo had been taken.

The reason I tell you all this is that I was looking from the wrong place.

What I needed to do, was heal myself before I started dating.

If I could have given myself some advice about where I was going wrong, it would be 'It's always an inside job.'

When you see negative patterns in your life, this is The Universe trying to demonstrate that you have something sitting beneath the surface that needs healing.

In my experience, particularly in working with women in business, it comes down to self-worth.

You see energetically, we vibrate at a certain frequency, and when you vibrate at a level of lack and scarcity, you attract men at the same frequency as you.

What I know now, is that the men I dated were alcoholics and abusive. One was adopted which sadly resulted in that he had low self-esteem (at a deep subconscious level, why could his mother abandon him?) and it was not until I cleared my internal blocks, that I'm Now able to see this with absolute clarity.

I've even seen and felt the shackles around the arms of some women that I've worked with, because of past life trauma where they have been shackled to a tree, or drowned for being a witch or healer.

Women throughout the ages have had a tough time of it, and if you feel drawn to do the work, then please reach out.

Most of my clients say that they knew that they needed to work with me, they just didn't know why.

It's not called Soul Psychology for nothing. Your soul connects to my soul and says, 'We need to work together.'

Many of my clients say to me, 'I knew that I had to work with you, the moment I met you.'

I spoke to a woman on the phone about a year ago about helping with my online dating. She promised that together we'd get to the bottom of what was going wrong, and she'd help me to create a top-notch dating profile so that I'd attract the right type of man, it was almost a dating coaching programme, what a great idea I thought!

Her marketing was excellent because I felt like she knew me.

I phoned her for a complimentary 20-minute conversation. She told me that the common themes with the men that I had a relationship with, were that they all put me in second place.

She was right of course, because of my low self-worth, something else always came first. What she wasn't doing was helping me to heal myself first and she was charging £10,000 for her package.

This encouraged me to go back over my dating history and look at the common themes.

Energy healing is like a muscle, as you practise it more and more, you become more intuitive, it becomes stronger, and now I feel it all over my body. I feel your blocks in my own body.

When I work with my clients, and they share their stories, I know where to explore with them. Using my tools, I can connect to my client, feel where their energy is blocked, and release it and give it back to the person that gave it to you, with love.

It's such a powerful yet gentle process.

I bought some beautiful angel wings that now sit on the wall behind me in my office. Physically, they represent what I feel, they also are a representation of my past. My wings hold the story of my past behind me so that I can move forward in my power.

These wings have now become something more than just a symbol. They are what people remember me for.

I've since started to use them in some of the communication tools that I use, as part of my personal brand.

Can you see the themes?

TASK

Go through all your serious relationships and write down the personality traits of these people.

Can you see a pattern? A theme?

It took me a long time to understand this. I was playing the victim. Why me? It's happened again.

Where are all the nice men? What's happening is that The Universe is reflecting men at you, who have the same personality traits. Because you still have some lessons to learn.

When your energy is high, when you vibrate from a place of joy and love, you attract similar types of people into your life.

When you vibrate from a place of scarcity and low self-esteem, guess what? That's exactly what reflects on you. He may be tall, dark, and handsome, but if he was treated badly as a child, let's say bullied, or he had a tough mother, abusive father, or adopted, the chances are that he will have some wounded child stories sitting beneath the surface.

What's the common theme with all these beautiful souls that you're dating?

And what can you do, to change it? I'll tell you. Do the inner work. Work on yourself, because the sooner you do this, the sooner you'll start to attract a better-quality soul mate.

CHAPTER NINE

Victim, or priestess - you choose

The story of the twins – why do you do what you do?

Long ago there were twin boys who had a drunken and abusive father.

He would be drinking in the chair every night, hitting their mother, and generally being a bullying alcoholic. As the twin boys grew, one left home as soon as he could. He scrimped and saved and got himself a clapped-out old banger and worked two jobs. He paid his way through University and met a lovely girl and had two boys. He was a successful entrepreneur.

The other brother stayed at home. He didn't work and started drinking at an early age. He met a girl and did exactly what his dad did to his mother.

When they were both asked why they were the way that they were, they said, 'My father.'

Can you see that you have a choice in life?

You can play the victim, or you can decide that this is not for me.

You decide. Do something about it. Change the programme that's been running in your family for generations.

Everyone is given the same opportunities, but it's up to you what you do with them. You can sit and watch TV every night. Catch up on soaps and be up to date with Love Island, or you can use those hours to make a better life for yourself and your family.

You choose.

The four levels of vibration

There are four levels of vibration.

Each one attracts certain things into your life.

Stage one – To me. – Victim Consciousness

We have all met people like this in our lives. Everything that happens to them is done by external sources. You'll hear them say things like. Why do I never seem to get a break in life? My partner treats me dreadfully. You might hear them say, 'It's not my fault. Everyone else is to blame.'

I operated in this stage for a large amount of my early adult life.

Stage two – By me. – Manifestor Consciousness

This is where you start to step up a gear. You're practising some spiritual practice. Starting to connect to your higher self, perhaps dabbling with the Law of Attraction.

Stage three - Through me – Channel Consciousness

You are connecting stronger with your spiritual practice. Manifesting much more and can see the benefit of this.

You start to relinquish to Spirit and see that everything happens for a reason.

Stage four is As Me. – Being Consciousness

Meditation is a large part of your daily routine. You feel connected to source. You have a feeling of total peace. Knowing that everything is mapped out in your life, exactly as it should be. You simply need to listen to the guidance that is being given to you.

TASK

YOUR THOUGHTS COME FIRST.

Here is a great exercise to do. It'll help you to see where your subconscious mind goes most of the time.

What are the five things you think about most?

I'd like you to write them down.

And then put a percentage next to them, about how much percentage per day you think about them.

Look at your list.

Then I'd like you to write what percentage is negative. For example

    My relationship - 65%

    Money and the lack of it - 75%

    My health - 60%

    Not owning my own home - 25%

> How my business is not taking off as I'd like it to - 85%

Then I'd like you to see how much of your thoughts are negative. This is such a powerful exercise.

And the reason for this is that your thoughts become things.

What I'd like you to do now, is take each one of those negative statements, for example

I'm worrying about how bad my relationship with my partner is and creating a defining moment.

Is it so bad that I can't continue?

Does it just need work, and can you see the potential of this relationship?

Do you spend more time with them that is good? Do you generally enjoy their company?

When I switch it, I'm 35% grateful for my relationship. There are lots of things that I love about it.

With money, I know that I'm always taken care of. I always have enough money to pay the bills. So rather than focusing on the negative, we start to focus on the positive.

And finally... am I prepared to do something about it?

But before you do, ask yourself, if I looked at this relationship through a different lens, what could it be like?

If I took one week to try my best to be a great partner, what could this relationship be?

Because it takes work to have a great relationship. Great relationships don't just happen overnight. No one is perfect.

When you focus on the negative side of your relationship, that's all you will see.

Why don't you take a week to focus on the positive personality traits that they have?

You went out with them for a reason, didn't you?

You attracted them for a reason.

Another piece of advice about relationships is:

Don't make a major decision until you've gone through all the seasons.

Go out with them for a year before you move in with them, buy a house together, etc. You need this time to see what this beautiful human is really like.

And finally, in my experience, don't give the essence of yourself away to someone else. This is also an indication of low self-worth. There is something very attractive about a strong independent woman who knows exactly where she's going and how she's going to get there. When you pin all your hopes and dreams on someone else's tailcoats, and then they're suddenly not there for a whole host of different reasons, you can lose all sense of purpose.

Depression is when you've got a blueprint of what life looks like and it's not going that way.

CHAPTER TEN

Searching for more Joy in my life

After I'd got through my first Christmas of losing my business I was struggling financially.

I needed money, and my foundational business background is in marketing.

I was so lost, and down that, I was searching for more joy in my life.

Then one morning a Facebook message dropped into my Inbox. It was from a lady who I'd met at a networking event about 4 years prior, and she asked if I was still doing marketing. She had written some empowering books for little girls, and could I help her market them?

I jumped at the chance. It was perfect for me, and what a beautiful subject.

I went over to her house, and I delivered my best piece of creative marketing strategy.

We started with a meditation.

We were sitting, cross-legged on her rug in the lounge. To encourage her to get that entrepreneurial chatter out of her head, I used Post It notes. This was so that I could put all her thoughts into, what I call, low-hanging fruit categories. To find the smart business offers that she had, to help her create income in the fastest possible route.

But we were interrupted. Her cat walked into the room and over the Post-It notes. It rubbed itself up against her and she said, 'I knew this would happen, we've got visitors.'

She told me that there was a group of my family here, she was a spiritual healer and they wanted to communicate with me. It took a little while to settle them down because they were all talking at once. 'Including' she said, 'someone who didn't have very nice energy,' who I think was my Step-Grandad.'

There was also my Great- Grandma on my mother's side, who, sadly, had taken her own life when my Grandma was 12, she was saying, 'Please forgive me, please forgive me.'

Finally, my Grandma stepped forward on my dad's side, who died when I was about 9. My memory of her was that she was quite a frail, tiny lady. She used to have her bed in the front room with a chamber pot beneath the bed.

We were living in South Africa at the time. It was in the days when you received a telegram of news overseas, which came from my Aunty. My dad's sister. She told us that Grandma had passed away. This was the first time I'd ever seen my dad cry.

As she came forward in Joy's sitting room, you could have drawn a line down the centre of my body. Because the whole left-hand side of my body started to tingle. My Grandma told me that she thought about me and my dad every day.

That I should be proud of what I'd been through because I was brave and come out of the other side, stronger.

That I had The Gift, and that I simply needed to decide to use it.

That I could do so much more than energy work. I just needed to choose.

And that, she would always be right there by my side and that, if I needed her, I had to hold her hand.

Because the left-hand side of my body was vibrating, I put my right hand on top of my left hand, and my left hand felt tiny! It was like I was holding my Grandma's hand. It was such a powerful, beautiful moment. And that moment, was when I stepped into the world of energy. There was no denying what I had just experienced. My life would never be the same again.

I currently have three spirit guides that help me with my healing work, and one of them is my Grandma. She stands at my left side, helping me. Guiding me.

Guess what the woman's name was who asked for my marketing support? Joy! Joy Fisher. I'd rediscovered the joy in my life.

CHAPTER ELEVEN

Setting up a smart business

My work story.

Because I had that belief in my head about 'you have to work hard for money,' I'd always worked hard for money. One of my core beliefs was, I'm one of life's 'get my sleeves rolled up' type of girl. I've always worked, right from the age of 14. I started with a paper round. Then I was promoted to Saturday girl in the shop. Then full time as an office administrator in a local haulage company. Now there's a story about a weird, crazy, power-hungry boxer guy, who walked around, even in the middle of winter in a T-shirt with a roll of banknotes in his back pocket. He ran a transport company, and on a Monday evening, we had to stay late to take orders over the phone from the reps.

We'd put them into date order to make sure that they were picked and packed at the right time, and then they'd be distributed across the UK.

One morning, he asked me to go into his office. He said, 'You've fucked up. You've put some of the orders in the wrong pile and you've cost me £300. So, for every £100 you've cost me. I'm going to smack your arse!

I went bright red. I couldn't believe what he was saying to me, but I didn't say a word.

And the best of it was, he told me that his bit on the side who worked there, was going to watch!

"We'll do it next Monday night in the warehouse after the staff had left," he said.

I was horrified!

I dwelled on it all week.

On Monday, I walked into his office, with my best Wonder Woman pose, gathered up every ounce of bravery that my little sixteen-year-old self could muster, and said, "My dad doesn't even do that to me, so you're not' and stormed out.

He then walked out of the office and said, "You're not fit to work in the office, so if you want a job, you're working in the warehouse."

Surprisingly, I didn't work there very long. I went back to college to do an art course. I loved it there. I did well. I was offered a place at Batley Art College to do fashion design but ended up getting pregnant with Daniel.

Setting up your own business

If you're in that beautiful stage of setting up your business, or you've got the luxury of time to create something new, I'd suggest that you make something that gives you residual income.

I know, I get it. Most women, particularly those that work in the healing world tell me that they can only do hands-on work. But Covid and lockdown put a stop to all that didn't it? We had to find a way to work remotely. And it was one of the best things that happened to us.

Don't linearly think about your business. Think about it holistically.

What are you passionate about? Could you teach what you already know?

Is it people, or is it the medium that you serve on, like TikTok, LinkedIn, email marketing, etc?

Or do you love video?

The message about how you must do it this way, or here's the next new thing. Or that you've got to be on it to make a difference, is all horse shit. Do what you love. If you're not comfortable talking to the camera. Don't do it.

You'll only look uncomfortable and unsure. It might come later as your confidence grows but you don't have to do everything. You'll disappear up your whatsit if you try to be everything to everyone.

Do one thing well.

Take it to market. See if people like it, then develop it further and get good at it.

It takes 100 hours to be a professional at something. You must do the work. But do it on one thing first and don't try and spread yourself too thinly.

The key is to get started. Do it messy, do it boldly, do it with courage and conviction, but start. The reason for this is that you won't know if it is what people want unless you start.

You might (like I did) create an online course. Spend 5 days with a challenge, and then not one person bought from me. No one! I was destroyed. All that work.

A beautiful friend of mine called Kayleigh Castle has spent some time working on herself and her business over the past couple of years.

Then she discovered TikTok. She's the queen of TikTok now. She talks about dating and self-worth, a subject that's close to my heart, and her message is loud and clear. She is forging ahead, and without playing and learning for the first couple of years, she wouldn't have found her groove.

If you are doing 121 work, make sure you charge your worth for it.

I know it's tricky when you're just starting out but be brave. I'm sure you could put your prices up by 10% and no one would even bat an eyelid.

Try it. See if it works and drop me a message to let me know that you did it.

Most truly successful entrepreneurs will have 6 or 7 different passive revenue streams.

I told myself this year that I will have three passive income products and of course one of them is my book.

I know that this seems obvious, and you may say to me, 'But Frances, everyone is doing it. The market seems so crowded with my field of expertise.' My darling, they're not doing it like you. Your perspective is that everyone is doing it. But you're in that field. There'll always be someone who needs what you have. They don't teach it like you. It won't land in their energy system as you do. They won't connect with another person as they do with you.

There's plenty to go around, you need to find your niche, and your niche is usually where your pain is. What is it that you've had to overcome to get you to where you are now?

You don't need to learn another skill or take another course. If you are two or three steps ahead of your target audience, you are the expert.

Because you teach what you need to learn the most

Because of the events in my life, I truly understand, deep down in my soul, how trauma and wounded child stories can affect women. Not just any women, but women who run their businesses, because your self-worth is your self-worth.

And if you haven't healed the stuck energy that sits beneath the surface, then you're not able to truly step up into that successful woman that you are meant to be.

Helping you to achieve huge growth by seeing what lies beneath your subconscious is my superpower.

Showing you how to set up a smart business, by feeling where your energetic blocks are, and at what age, so that together we can release them and give them back to the person that gave them to you, is my superpower.

Together, we work on what's going on inside and outside, so that nothing gets in your way.

One of the tools that I've learned along the way, to help you have empowering conversations is the

3 x F formula.
- Facts
- Feels
- Future

This is particularly good for when you need to have a conversation about something that's upsetting you, and you don't want your emotions to get in the way.

The first stage is to make sure that you're in a great state, and by that, I mean you're not still caught up in any negative energy. If someone has made you mad, then sleep on it, or go for a walk. Or wait until the next time you see them, so that the dust has settled.

You need to be energy neutral.

It's important because you don't want to go straight into the conversation feeling on edge. If this happens, you'll probably drop straight into defence mode, and you need to be in control of both your energy and emotions.

Let's use an example:

You have a friend who is always late, and it is starting to get on your nerves.

Start with the first F – FACTS

What are the facts?

Whenever we meet up, you are late. Don't use the word always unless that is a fact.

Last time you were 15 minutes late. And the time before that you were 30 minutes late.

Only use facts at this stage.

The second F - FEEL

How it makes you feel. This is important because no one can argue about the way you feel.

It makes me feel that you don't value my time. That you think you're more important than me.

That you're happy for me to stand outside in the cold waiting for me.

I get angry or upset. Whatever the emotion is that you feel when this happens.

And the final F - FUTURE

What you'd like to happen in the future?

You might say something like, 'The next time we meet, I'd like you to arrive at the time we've agreed.

Simple!

You'll be amazed at how this works. I love it because it's simple.

I've witnessed hundreds of women use this formula for all types of conversation. Including their partners, children, and work colleagues. It's a simple yet powerful tool.

CHAPTER TWELVE

Finding your GIFT - everyone has a gift and a medicine

When Bird Board folded it was devastating, and I didn't see it. At the time, I still had healing lessons to learn, so that I could become the woman I am today.

When you're hurting because something negative has happened, sometimes you're so in the thick of it that you can't see what you need to learn. I was approached by a beautiful soul called David Taylor, who is a coach and filmmaker, and he asked me if I'd like to join him in a safe space to talk and make a film.

At the time I wasn't sure how it would help, but through that process, he encouraged me to see some of the beautiful gifts that I had helped to create, whilst the business was flourishing.

One of them was the Shoe Box Appeal.

I've attached a link here so that you can see the raw emotion that sat behind the interview. That process was so valuable https://vimeo.com/uncontained/shoebox

It taught me so many things.

1. You must dive deep to climb high.
2. The gift of giving is a powerful thing.
3. Being raw and vulnerable helps connect you to everything.

I believe that everyone has a gift and a medicine.

Your gift is what you were put on this earth to do.

Your medicine is how you share it with the world.

There will be four of five key things that have happened in your life, that have shaped the woman that you are today.

Write them down. Remember the story about the twins? Did you rebel against them, or did you absorb them and re-enact those personality traits? Everything that has happened to you has shaped you in some way, shape, or form.

The Universe will reward you for sharing your gift with the world. Especially if it helps people. Do it as an act of service, and you will be rewarded.

When we do things from a place of love, everything opens up for us. Life will become joy-filled, and easy. This is because it's meant to be.

You don't have to be an expert at your chosen path, you simply need to be two or three steps ahead of your target audience.

Becoming a teacher means you're deep diving into your field of expertise and when you're teaching, you know that you need to have the answers for your clients, so you'll learn even faster.

One of the many lessons I've learnt in my years of running my own business is that I stopped too soon because of my limiting beliefs.

I've spent thousands of pounds on courses. Each one is in a different field of expertise.

I'd start, with a challenge, or an online course, spending hours planning and prepping, and marketing, to not have one person sign up.

It was soul-destroying. And I'd give up.

If you're feeling like that, then keep going. There'll be something that needs tweaking and changing.

Do the research. Is it what they want? Is the outcome absolutely crystal clear? Are you telling them about the results they get?

If you feel like you're marketing too much, I can promise you that you're not. Double your marketing, triple it.

Don't fear marketing. It's like having a beautiful car, parked in the garage, if you don't take it out and drive it, and show it off, then no one is going to feel the benefit of it are they?

Act as if you're being paid £100,000 salary for being the Marketing Manager of your business. Because you will be someday.

Don't lose faith, and don't lose sight of what you are here to cause and create. It will come.

Remember that if things don't go the way you thought they were going to go, then, there's a lesson for you to learn somewhere.

CHAPTER THIRTEEN

Client Stories

Everything happens in our lives for a reason.

I believe that everything that happened to me, was so that I can help women heal.

Money, men, and energy are all connected.

What happens in one area, reflects in another.

If, like me, you feel that you are going round and round in circles, with business, with money, with relationships. At some level you are sabotaging your growth, then these are all indications that you have blocked energy in your system.

Because of the life I've lived, nothing shocks me.

I have been told that I must write my book, because there are thousands of women standing behind me, waiting for me to write it.

When I heard that statement, I knew at my deepest soul level that it was true.

The biggest challenge that women have is their self-belief and confidence. We are taught from being little girls to be nice, help our siblings, and speak when we're spoken to. Our value was based on the way that we look, not who we are as a person, which slowly erodes our confidence and self-worth, so much so that we believe it at our core.

We play safe by being in our feminine energy.

Feminine energy is that beautiful creative, safe space where we dream and nurture.

Masculine energy is the go-getter. The salesperson, hitting targets, achieving life's ambitions.

The problem with this is that we've been taught to live in a masculine environment all our lives, and this is not where we are in our zone of genius. A sort of a do or die mentality.

I've gone through this journey, running huge businesses, and wearing suits. I headed a marketing agency; coached women from all types of professions listened to their challenges and had the privileged to watch them flourish and grow when they realised, that life doesn't have to be this way. Most times, this realisation happens when we reach burnout.

When we connect to our powerful feminine, she helps us rise. Without the stress and the burnout.

Let me tell you that it is not pink, fluffy, woo-woo stuff with affirmations and meditations, you still have to do the work. It can be messy, painful, and downright ugly, but when you get through the other side, you'll see a place of knowing your true calling. It feels almost effortless.

Energy healing is intangible. It's a feeling, that you can't quite put your finger on, and it's so powerful.

Women are meant to connect to their femininity, it is where our power is.

When you find yourself going round and round in circles, making similar mistakes, that's usually the first indicator that you have blocked energy. Energy healing helps get you back to your pure energetic blueprint. So that you can be the person that you were meant to be.

What I see when I first work with my clients is that there can be a lot of victim mentality within their belief system. For example, why does this always happen to me? How come I see other women around me running wonderful, successful businesses, and I can't seem to get mine off the ground?

In energy work, children choose their parents for the lessons they need to learn in life. My parents weren't great role models. But really, our parents are all simply doing the best that they could with what they had. It is their learnt behaviour too. They didn't have the tools, that we have. To be able to break through the cycles of self-destruction and limiting beliefs that keep us stuck. They learned their behaviours from their parents, and their parent's parents. If you think about it, over the last century, we have had two world wars, which means most of our beliefs come from a place of lack and having to make do and mend.

But our world is not like this now.

If you have a laptop and a connection to the internet, the world is your oyster. You can create anything that you want if you want it bad enough. You simply need to believe that you can.

Natalie's Story

Natalie reached out to me because she wanted to cleanse her body on a physical, spiritual, and emotional level.

She told me that she had grown up in a religious family. Almost cult-like, and everything that she believed about money and love came through these religious filters.

She had also experienced sexual assault by two family members.

She told me that she was not able to express her feelings and emotions and experienced pain during sex.

During our sessions together we looked at masculine and feminine energy, prosperity, and her four lower bodies. The core emotion that was less than optimal, was indignation.

When we look up the meaning of this word it means 'showing anger at what is perceived as unfair treatment.'

After one of the sessions when I contacted Natalie to see how she was feeling she told me, "I'm going to Wales on a family holiday, and normally I'd be panicky and anxious. I feel like I've let go of the shame about my weight and my body. Also, the pain during sex has gone!"

Colin's Story

(not his real name)

Colin was 17 when he first came to see me. He was a voluntary mute; he chose not to speak. Because of energy work, I don't need my clients to talk to me, as I feel into their energy.

Doing my work, I can tell you how old you were when you took the negative energy on, where it is in your body, and who gave it to you.

Colin was about to go off to college to learn how to be a computer programmer.

So his mum wanted him to have the best start on this new chapter of his life.

As I've said before, I believe that everyone has a gift, and everyone has a medicine. Your gift is what makes you uniquely you, and your medicine is how you share it with the world.

At around session four, I said to Colin, 'What If your gift is that you were meant to be mute and that your medicine is that you're meant to create a piece of software that helps people to communicate?

His whole face lit up!

It was like he'd found his purpose. It was a beautiful moment…

What I discovered, when I tested to see where the energy was stuck in his system was that at the age of two, his grandfather had abused him and he'd told him to keep it a secret. To keep it quiet. At the age of two, we are just starting to formulate our language. Imagine what a huge impact that had on his life, at such a young age. He had quite literally done that and chose not to speak to anyone apart from his mum.

Catherine's Story

Catherine came to me with a money issue. Low self-worth manifested in not charging enough for her high-end services.

She is a wonderful creative. A textile designer with years of experience under her belt. When we met and talked about money, I knew that she had money blocks.

We did an energy medicine session together. I sent her a questionnaire that asked her things about her conscious beliefs about money.

I was able to read into this energy and this enabled us to hit the ground running during our session together.

What we uncovered was that her energy was low. She is an empath which means that she easily absorbs other people's energy. What was fascinating was that when I tested to see where these blocks had originated, they had been passed through her DNA lineage. From three generations ago.

She told me that her Great Grandma had been adopted, and adoption can create unconditional love issues. None of this energy belonged to Catherine; it had been absorbed into her system through her DNA.

When I felt into her energy to see where it was stuck, it was in her hara, (her womb) which is her creative centre.

For those of you that already work with energy, you'll know that our feminine energy is the creative energy, and masculine energy is the action-taking energy.

I spoke to Catherine a few days after our session, and she told me that she felt more confident. She said, 'the energy she felt during the session was uplifting like she was glowing from within, and the positivity and confidence were just so abundant.'

She felt like her old self. Like her inner child had come out to play, and as you can imagine, that's important when you're a creative!

And finally… guess what? She said, "I've had someone get in touch to place not one, but two commissions for designs!"

Emma's Story

When Emma came to me, she was looking for help about how to support herself and how she could be a great mum to her son who has special needs.

She booked a block of six sessions, and during the first session, we were able to get to the core of what was needed for her, and her relationship with her son.

She told me that after that first session, she felt stronger, more in control, and able to stand up and ask external providers for what he needed.

We then started to work on Emma's personal needs around being a great business owner, and her energetic gifts.

We worked on subjects such as

1. Making empowering choices

2. Fulfilling her full potential

3. Integrating her masculine and feminine energy

The journey with Emma was beautiful, I felt privileged to witness her gentle unfolding.

Emma's glands were blocked, and when your glands are blocked it means that you are unable to communicate with your soul. By releasing this block, her true soul calling was evident for all to see.

She also had a belief that being successful was a negative thing.

That it created stress and overwhelm, and that people didn't like you if you were successful.

When we explored this in more detail during our last session, I helped Emma to see that she could choose her version of success. And it didn't need to be anyone else's story.

Emma is a spiritual, intuitive woman and her feminine energy was blocked. To not use that gorgeous feminine energy to its full, felt like such a waste of talent. I crafted a healing session that helped her to balance her masculine and feminine so that she could fulfill her potential. Emma's journey was a slower one, because everyone goes at the right speed for them. This gave her the time to put into practise the things that unfolded for her.

Her confidence is growing day by day.

Barbara's Story

Barbara is an author and came to me because she was struggling with 'unconditional love issues.

During each session, we looked at one element of her emotional body.

During her first two sessions, she had huge shifts in her energy. She was releasing something strong that was getting in the way of her growth.

I reassured her that we had to go deep to release whatever was sitting beneath the surface.

She told me that she'd had a fabulous opportunity to write a book that her daughter inspired her to write. It felt like The Universe was conspiring to put all the elements in place for her so that she could be her ultimate creative self. To live her life purpose.

Every session with Barbara was about her emotional language.

We looked at her emotional meridians, and her glands (because they communicate with your soul), and her soul purpose.

Like a cobweb, we peeled away the emotional blocks, layer by layer.

Emotions connect to your creativity because this is your feminine energy. Your Hara (your womb) is the physical store cupboard of your creativity. As we shifted Barbara's energy, I could feel a heavy weight in my hara, as I connected to her energetically. Something was leaving her, for good!

As she shared this story with me, I already knew that this book was going to be a huge success.

My spirit guides told me so.

When you dive deep beneath the surface, most of us are living our lives at the surface level. Almost on autopilot.

True gold lives beneath the surface in our subconscious. It is where we have automatic belief systems running.

Just like me, where I did not understand unconditional love, this manifests in not feeling worthy, and not valuing yourself. This then plays out in every area of your life. If it were a quick fix, we would all do this work because it is so powerful, but the complexity comes because we are all unique, with slightly different beliefs and nuances that sit beneath the surface.

These beliefs affect every single area of your life, from personal relationships to how you show up for work. Particularly if you run your own business.

Because everything is an inside job. The greatest piece of work you can do is to work on your self-belief and self-worth, it will reap so many rewards for you at every single level.

Doing the inner work is not a one-and-done thing. It's like a spider's web, and as you release the first layer, it will help to release the second. Until you get to the core of what's holding it all in place. Your wounded child stories. These stories don't have to be terrible. We all have them. Even if you have amazing parents who loved you, there will still be some areas of belief, that keep you playing small.

Common ones are things like:

- You must work hard to be successful.
- You must start at the bottom and work your way up.
- Success makes you a bitch.
- Good men are not attracted to successful women.
- Nice people aren't successful.
- There are no nice men out there.
- I'm rubbish at relationships.
- There is never enough money/time.

Does any of this sound familiar to you?

They're simply not true.

They're all limiting beliefs that we store in our energy system, that keep us playing small.

Imagine what your life could be like if you released all those blocks that are playing out beneath the surface.

A voyage of self-discovery that will unlock many keys for you. Your success is waiting for you.

Come and meet your inner child. She holds the secrets to your success.

Everything is an inside job. Once you release the limiting beliefs that you have, you can set yourself free from the energy shackles that bind you.

Your true success lies beneath the surface. You can take all the action steps you like and build a great big business. You can become successful, but sooner or later, your inner child will come out to play and remind you that you still have work to do. She shows herself in unusual ways. And always when you're not feeling great. That's when the self-doubt and the negative inner dialogue begins.

When we do the inner work, everything changes forever. When your energy shifts and changes, nothing is ever the same again. You start to embody a new more powerful reality, and that's where real change happens.

Epilogue

I knew I had to write this book.

I've had people tell me that they didn't want me to write it, because they weren't comfortable with the personal information that I would be sharing with the world, but I had to write it.

I was told by a powerful Shaman, that there were thousands of women standing behind me that needed me to write this book.

That was meaning enough for me, to create it. It reinforced the message that I received loud and clear.

Write the book.

It almost confirmed to me, that all those experiences throughout my life, were not meaningless. That I had to go through them to truly understand what it meant to be broken and lost, and then find my way home. As I write this, I have tears of joy, flowing down my cheeks. I know that the healing journey is never truly complete, and that it is a lifetime's work, but I'm so much more healed than I was.

The book has been sitting waiting for me, for quite some time, but it wasn't until I realised that it wasn't just my story, and that if it became a self-help book, that the momentum began to shift.

Energetically, when we are of service to the world. Spirit will step in, and support you, with what you do.

You can call it karma, The Universe, God, whatever you believe in, it's still a higher realm.

I believe that by adding the extra layer of self help to the book, gave it, its purpose.

I feel that it's my life's work to become a better healer, so that I can help women all over the world, to heal themselves.

By writing the book, I discovered my purpose. It helped me heal.

You know that phrase, 'When the student is ready, the teacher will come.' That's exactly what happened with me.

I was on holiday; bored, and thought to myself, now would be a good time, to start writing a couple of chapters of my book. I wrote every day. Even on the plane on my way home. It just simply seemed to flow.

By the way, you may be curious about whether I'm in a happy and healthy relationship now.

I can confirm that I am.

The man that I'm with now, is a direct reflection of me.

He is kind, supportive, and a completely different man, to the men that I attracted in the past.

Acknowledgments

I want to thank each and every man that I've had a relationship with.

If they read this book, then I hope they don't take the words that I've written too personally. I've simply written it from my experience, and of course everyone remembers things from a different perspective.

I had some big lessons to learn, and they helped me to learn them. I didn't listen to the messages that were being given to me over and over again. You had your job to do, to help me heal. Thank you.

I want to thank the group of beautiful women who have supported me on my journey of becoming a healer, coach and author. I quite honestly, don't know what I would have done without you. You've been there for me, listened to me. Hugged me and most importantly, not judged me. Thank you.

To my beautiful family. You supported me through thick and thin. You've financially, emotionally, and physically been there when I needed you.

To my children – I know I wasn't the best mum to you but know that I love you with all my heart.

To my grandchildren, I feel that I get a second chance, knowing what I know now, to be an amazing grandma. To be there for you, in a way that I wasn't for your parents.

I love you all.

Additional Resources

Stay in touch

Facebook group https://www.facebook.com/groups/everythingisenergy01/

Linkedin https://www.linkedin.com/in/francesdayceo/

If you'd like to find out how you can work with Frances head onto her website at **www.frances-day.co.uk**

For a free Visualisation Meditation visit
subscribepage.io/Visualisation

Bibliography

- Louise Reed – Energy Shaman - Energy Medicine Institute – Australia
  https://energymedicineinstitute.com.au/

- Lynn Robinson - Spiritual healer
  https://www.lynn-robinson-spiritual-hub.co.uk/

- Sarah Negus – A modern Day Shaman
  www.sarahnegus.com

- Lenka Lutonska – Energetic Selling and marketing
  https://www.lenkalutonska.com/

About the Author

Frances is an energy healer and soul coach. She has run multiple businesses from scratch. All with a similar theme, women in business.

Her biggest success to date was Bird Board. With over 150 members belonging to 15 boards, along the M62 corridor in the North of England. Bird Board was a mastermind group where women met monthly to help each other with their personal and business challenges. This is where she learned her coaching skills.

She has been a chartered marketer, running a marketing agency in Leeds and more recently an energy healer. Blending her skills to help coach and heal women in business, so that they step into who they are truly meant to be. She specialises in healing self-worth blocks and wounded child stories.

She blends these skills today to help women in business be their most amazing selves.

Facebook.com/FrancesDayCoach
Instagram.com/francesdaycoach
Linkedin.com/in/francesdayceo

Printed in Great Britain
by Amazon